Table of Contents

Enlarging Patterns

The bulletin board patterns in this book may be enlarged to the size that most closely fits the bulletin board on which they will be placed. You can enlarge these objects by using an opaque projector, overhead projector, or copy machine.

If using an overhead projector, make a transparency of the pattern with a transparency maker or use an overhead pen to trace the pattern onto a sheet of clear acetate. Tape a sheet of paper or tagboard on the wall. Place the transparency on the overhead projector, and move the projector forward or backward until the image on the wall is the desired size. To achieve a mirrored image of a pattern, simply turn the transparency over. Trace around the projected image, then use crayons, water pastels, colored chalk, or marking pens to complete the sketch. Cut out the picture, label it with a suggested caption or one of your own, and attach it to the bulletin board. (Note: If you are using an opaque projector, you do not need to trace the pattern onto acetate before enlarging.)

If the pattern needs to be only a bit larger than the original, use a copy machine. Some machines are capable of enlarging as much as 200 percent at one time. Become familiar with your copy machine beyond exact duplications—it can be a valuable resource.

General Suggestions

Use small, blank patterns to turn bulletin boards into interactive games; to display student work; to make an incentive board, etc. Each bulletin board has unlimited possibilities to become a learning tool in your classroom.

Obtaining Materials for the Bulletin Board

Finding materials to create your bulletin boards can be fun for you and your class and can also be a way to meet members of your community. You may even want to coordinate the pick-up of donated materials with a field trip! Emphasize the concept of recycling with your students as you collect donated materials. Designate a space in your room to store the materials. Involve other teachers and classes so the school builds its supply of materials and props for various school functions. Below is a list of ideas to get you started.

- Collect magazines from medical offices and ask students to bring some from home.
- Ask decorating and wallpaper stores for discontinued paper sample books and tiles.
- Fabric stores may contribute remnants. They also sell beads and buttons by bulk.
- Local newspapers may give roll ends of newsprint away when they have become too small to use. Printing companies may also have leftover scraps of paper.
- Visit yard sales and flea markets for inexpensive costumes, props, and decorations.
- Ice cream stores may provide round containers that can make storage containers, musical instruments, and three-dimensional art projects.
- Grocery stores and discount chain stores have large cardboard boxes and packing materials. They may also have clear plastic bubble wrap that can be used as water.
- Always ask parents if they have anything they can donate from work or hobbies.
- Buy wrapping paper, especially foil, on sale after Christmas for use as bulletin board backgrounds.

Let your apple bulletin board introduce a bushel of fall fun with creative writing topic choices. Duplicate and enlarge the patterns on pages 4, 5 and 6 to create an "a-peeling" classroom display. Write fall topics such as "Autumn Leaves," "My First Day of School," or "The Apple Gang" on apple patterns, then let the writing fun begin.

Additional Uses

- Use apples to highlight student work.
- Welcome students to school by writing their names on apples.
- Display book jackets for "choice" books to read.
- Read the story of Johnny Appleseed, then display apple seeds on the apples.
- Have students graph their favorite types of apples on the bulletin board.

Finishing Touches

- Construct the basket with a brown paper bag stuffed with newspapers.
- Cut the apple patterns from red felt.
- Place apple potpourri in a small basket nearby.
- Use red twist paper to form a border.
- Have students color apple patterns, then display around the board as a border.

Creative Captions

- Harvesting a Great Bunch
- Bushels of Good Work
- A is for "A-Peeling" Work
- Let's Have a Bushel of Fun!
- You Are the Apple of My Eye!
- Bushels of Books
- Plant the "Seed" of an Idea
- Fall into a Basketful of Fun!

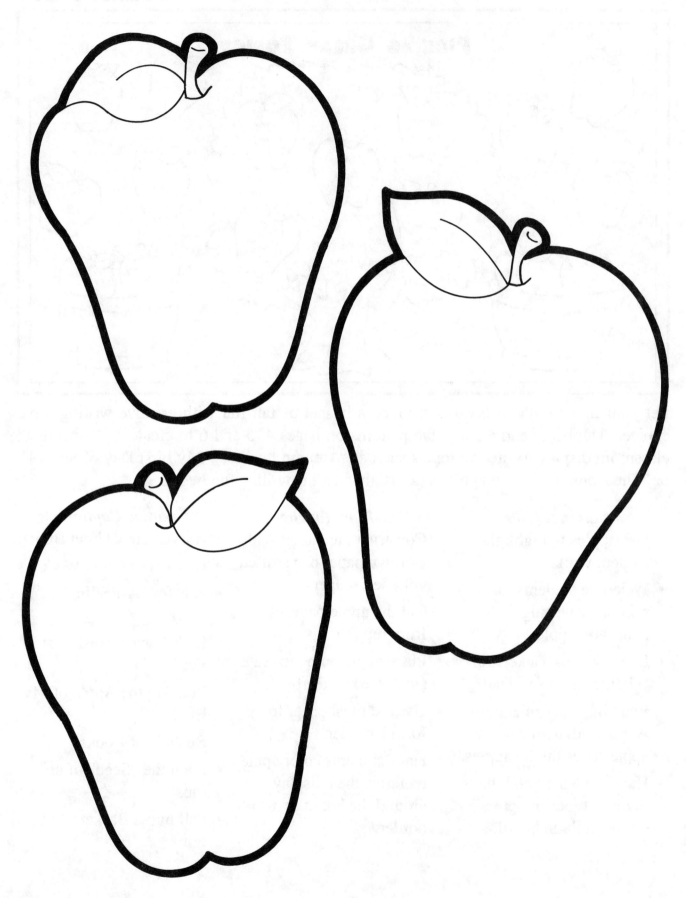

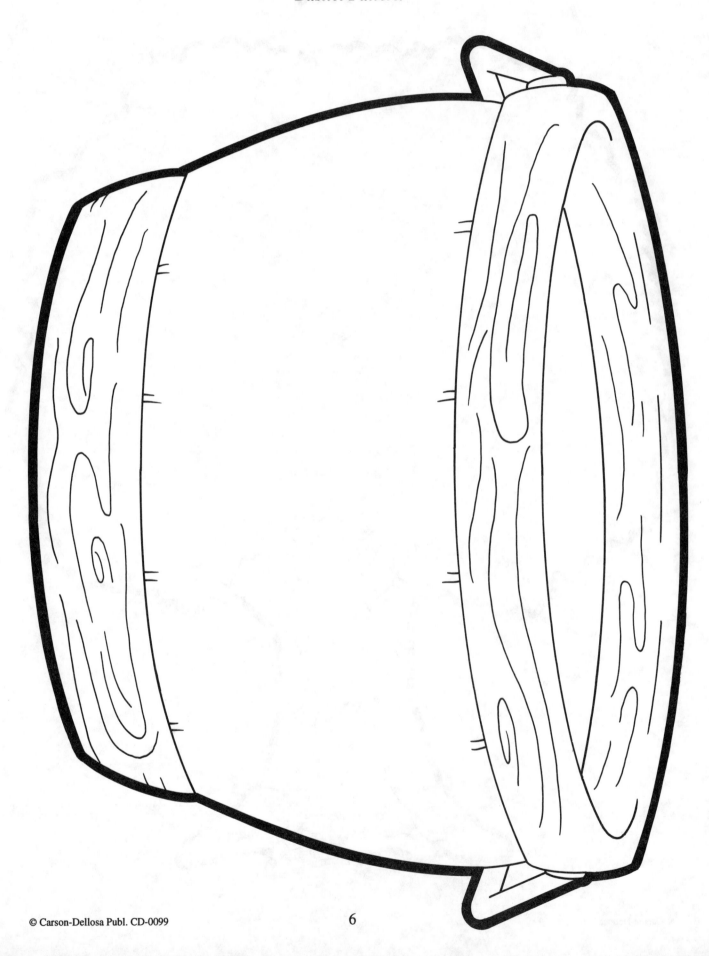

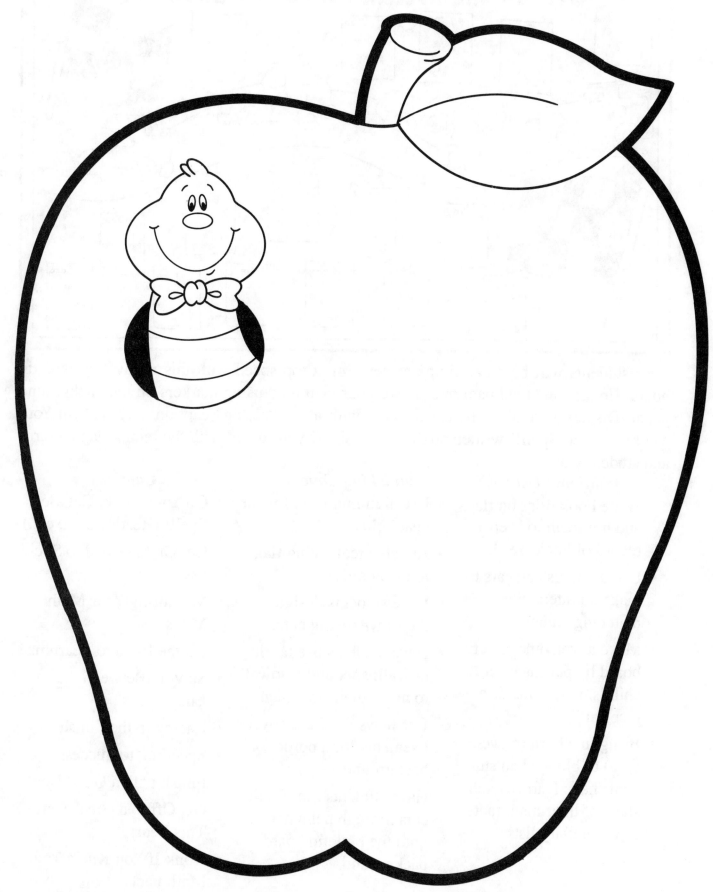

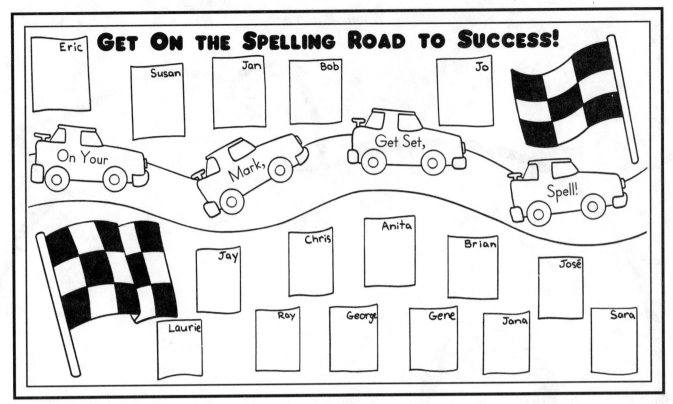

Your students will be "revved up" to perform at top speed with this motivating bulletin board. Enlarge the road pattern or make your own road using markers on the background paper. Display several of the car patterns with a fun "racing" caption such as "On Your Mark, Get Set, Spell!" written on them. Finish off your board with the racing flag patterns and student work.

Additional Uses

- Write book titles on flags and use them to keep a record of books read.
- Use the flags and cars to make an interactive matching game.
- Make a welcome bulletin board by putting each child's picture inside a race car.
- Bring in a horn (bicycle type) to blow when students have learned each stage of their math facts or vocabulary lists.

Finishing Touches

- Use aluminum foil for car headlights.
- Attach a real racing flag to the board.
- Have students design their own racing cars.
- Have students use fabric or wallpaper and a dowel to make their own flags.
- Use newspaper car advertisements for a border or background.
- Have students run plastic cars through paint and onto the bulletin board background.

Captions

- On Your Mark, Get Set, Spell! (Read, Count, etc.)
- Get On the Road to Success
- Measuring Your Math Miles
- On the Road to Learning
- Staying Between the Lines
- Racing to the Finish
- Speeding to Success
- Finish with a Good Book
- Get Off to a Great Start This Year!
- Honk If You Know Your Math Facts

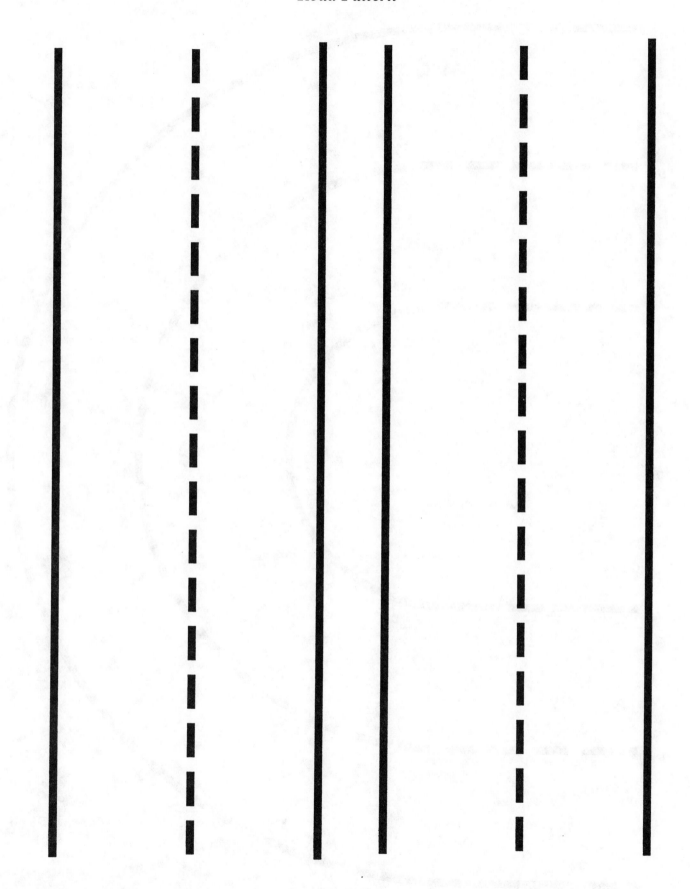

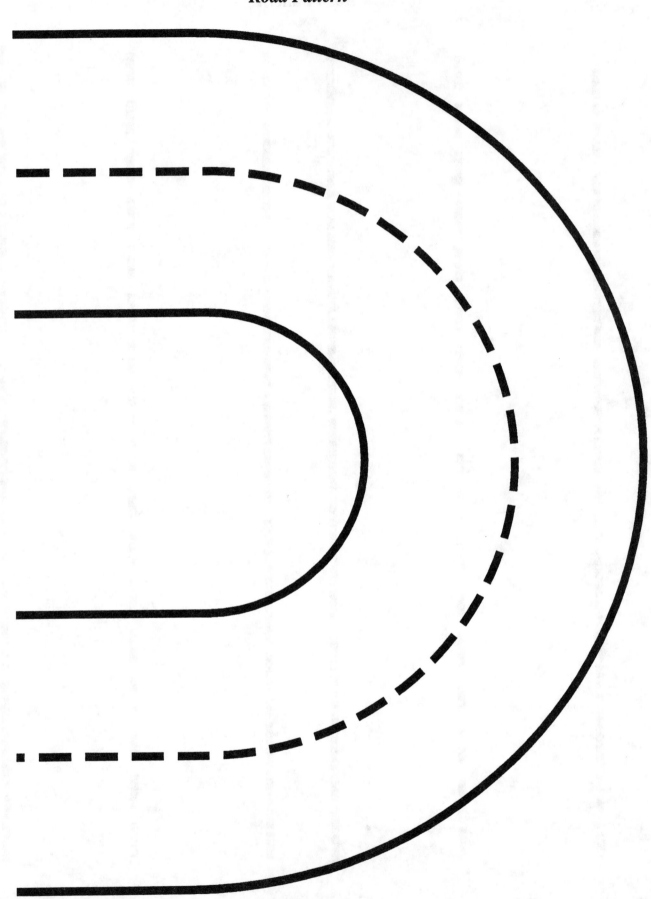

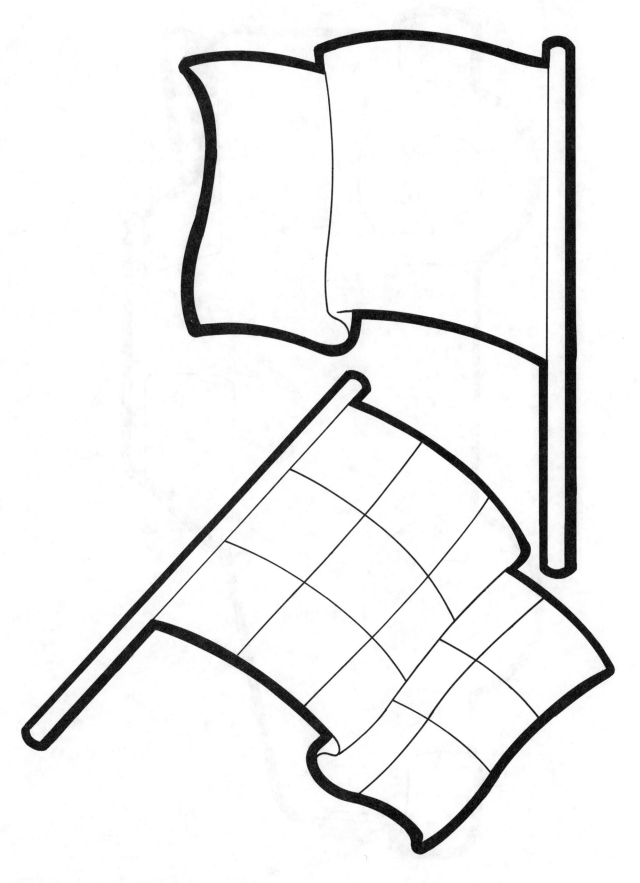

11

Racing Car Pattern

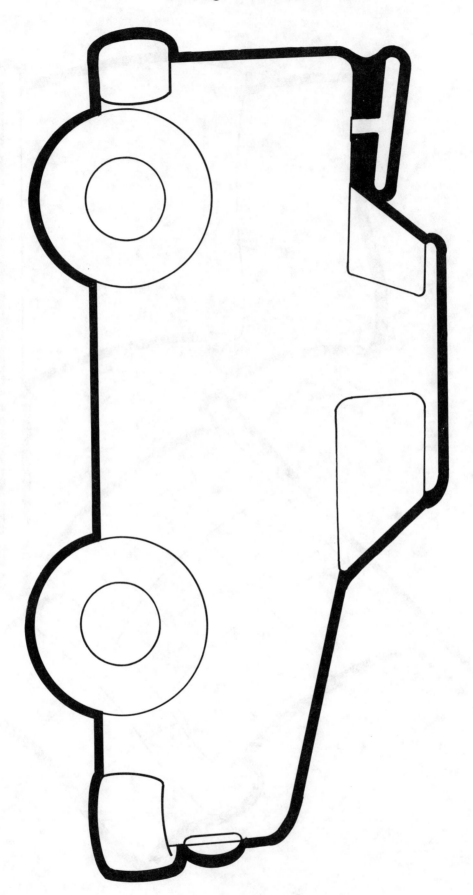

THE BEST

Anne · Ed · Dan · Betsy · Jake · Mark · Jesse · Katie · Chris · Marie · Lee · Lynn · John · Sue · José · Jan · Bob · Joe

OF THE BUNCH!

This bulletin board is a "grape" way to welcome students to a new class. Enlarge the pattern on page 14 to fit the classroom door. Write student names on the grapes. Attach the bunch of grapes to your door and use construction paper or twist paper to make a vine. Title the board, "The Best of the Bunch!"

Additional Uses

- Have students graph their favorite types of grapes on the bulletin board.
- Use the board as a "Things that are Purple" display. Have students cut out magazine pictures of things that are purple and place them on the bulletin board with the grapes.
- Use the bulletin board to display "gr" blend words such as grape, green, grandfather, grill, etc.
- Use the grapes as a centerpiece for a "Good Fruits" nutrition bulletin board.

Finishing Touches

- Make a vine out of twist paper.
- Use wood to make a trellis.
- Obtain plastic grapes to use on the vine or trellis.
- Use purple balloons as grapes.
- Put students' pictures on purple construction paper "grapes."
- Use grape juice labels or cans as a border.

Captions

- The Best of the Bunch
- Ripe for Reading
- Good Books by the Bunch
- "Grape" Work
- We Are Hanging Together
- Grape Vine Time
- Be a Part of the Bunch
- "Grape" News
- Dropping in With a Bunch of Good News
- Learning is Delicious

Basket Pattern

17

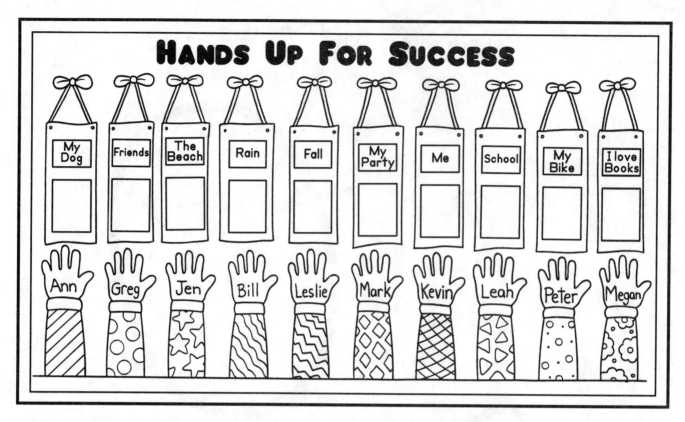

Your students can show their best efforts on this "Hands Up for Success" bulletin board. Enlarge the arm pattern on page 22, and give each student a copy. Have each student decorate the arm to look like his own. Display each students' work above his arm. Ribbon can be added above the classwork for a nice finishing touch. This idea can be modified to use with the footprint and shoe patterns on pages 20 and 21.

Additional Uses

- Use real book jackets for a "Sneaking Up on Good Books" bulletin board.

- Make an interactive game matching hands to feet or feet to sneakers.

- Let each child choose colored paper that matches his skin to make arms for the board.

- Use the hands for a "Helping Hands" board to display ways children can help in the community.

Finishing Touches

- Use real socks on the bulletin board.

- Use fabric or wallpaper for the clothing on the arms.

- Hang real balloons on the board.

- Allow students to make hand and foot prints on the butcher paper and use the paper as a background.

- Bring in shoelaces and tie them into bows to use as a border.

Creative Captions

- Lending a Hand

- Hands Up for a Great Year

- Reach for the Stars

- Reach for Success

- Stretch the Distance for Math

- Jump into Reading

- Kick Your Feet Up

- Hand in Hand We Learn

- Put Your Best Foot Forward

- Hands Up for a Great Adventure

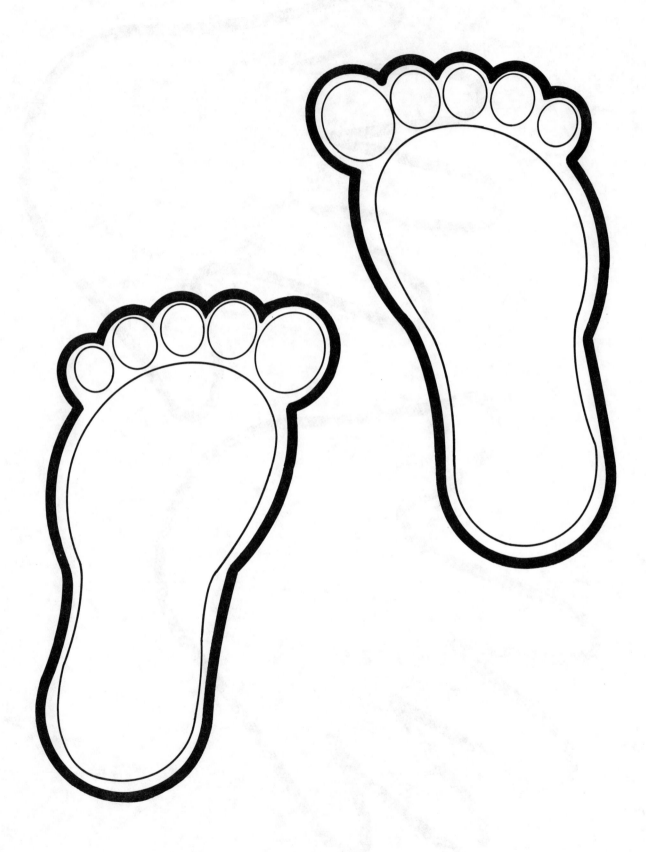

Shoe Pattern

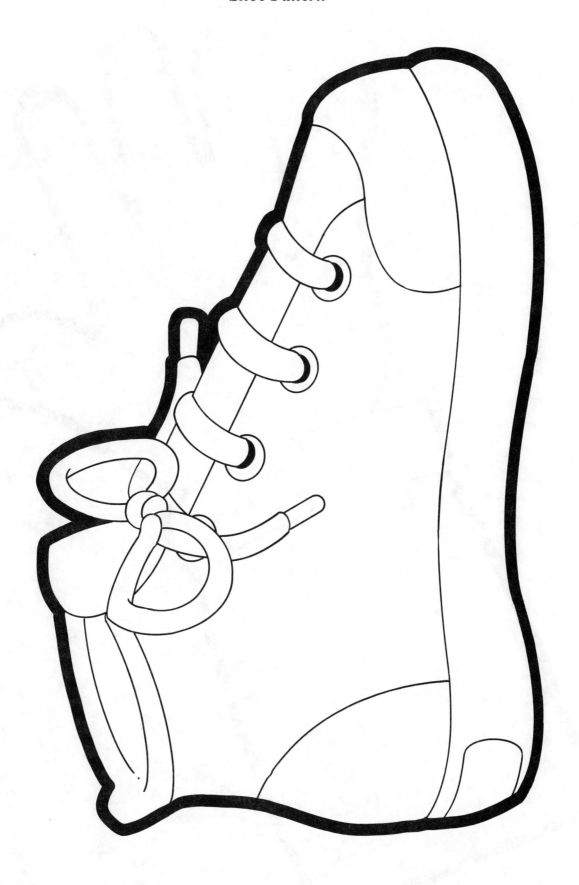

21

STICK TO THE RULES

Classroom rules won't be a "sticky" subject when introduced with this decorative bulletin board. Enlarge the gumball machine, boy pattern and girl pattern from pages 24, 25 and 26. Display the characters around the gumball machine. Write classroom rules on individual gumballs. Use gum wrappers as a border. Substitute the dog pattern on page 27 for the boy or girl pattern if you desire.

Additional Uses

- Give each child a copy of the page 24 gumball machine to use as an individual incentive chart.
- Put students's pictures onto construction paper circles that represent gum balls.
- Graph each students' favorite gum or candy.
- Display a jar of gumballs in front of the bulletin board. Have students estimate how many pieces are in the jar.

Finishing Touches

- Attach round balloons to represent bubble gum on the bulletin board.
- Use gum wrappers as a border.
- Use foil to cover the bottom of the gumball machine to make it look like metal.
- Use plastic wrap to cover the top of the gumball machine.
- Use the coin patterns from page 129 to display around the gumball machine.

Creative Captions

- Stick to Good Behavior
- Stretch Your Imagination
- We're on the Ball
- Sweet Taste of Success
- Blowing Bubbles
- Smacking of Great Ideas
- Estimate
- Reading is a Bubble-Blowing Experience
- Reading Adds Flavor to Life
- Goody, Goody Gum Balls!
- Pop into a Good Book

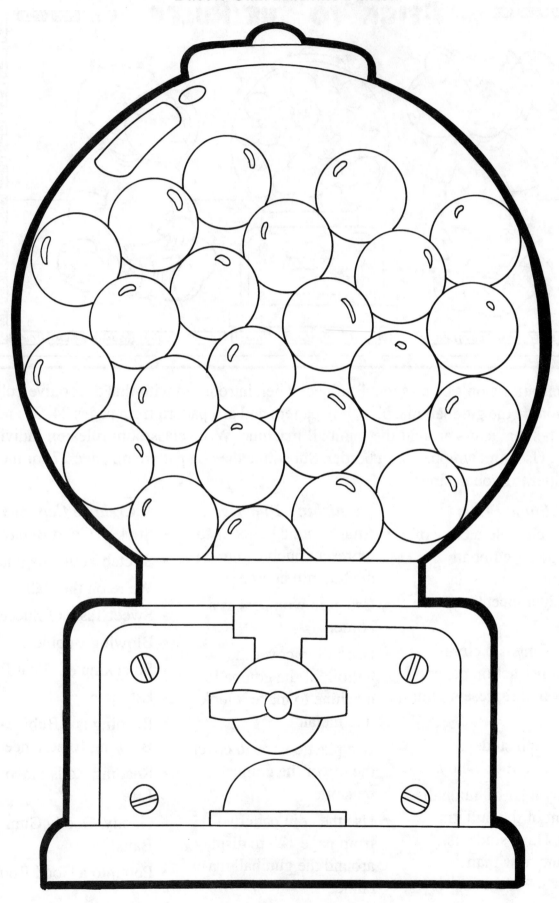

DIALING GOOD SAFETY RULES

Give the message to your students, "Be Safe!" Enlarge the phone and receiver pattern on page 29. List safety rules on copies of the page 30 pattern and display on the board. This bulletin board can be an interactive teaching tool for a unit on safety or as a backdrop to display student work. The Phone Directory pattern on page 31 can be personalized with student's names and phone numbers.

Additional Uses

- Bring in a real telephone and set it up in front of the bulletin board for students to practice good phone manners.
- Have children practice dialing their phone numbers and emergency numbers.
- Have students locate their names in a phone book.
- Make a "Person-to-Person" bulletin board matching up student buddies/study mates.
- Make a communication bulletin board listing all the ways people communicate.

Finishing Touches

- Use a phone cord as a border.
- Mount old telephone directory pages on the bulletin board as a background.
- Display safety and emergency phone numbers for your area.
- Use curling ribbon to make phone cords.
- Use real message pad sheets as a border.
- Have students cut out pictures of phones from magazines and use as a border.

Captions

- Calling All Good Citizens/Learners
- Dial "M" for Math
- Practice Good Phone Manners
- Ring in the New Year
- Call Your Teacher When You Need Help
- Buzz a Good Friend
- Ringing in Good Study Habits
- Calling on a Good Book
- Person to Person
- Dialing Good Safety Rules
- We Know Our Phone Numbers

While You Were Out

SETTING THE STAGE FOR GOOD WORK

Show off your "Star Performers" on this stage for good work. Enlarge the boy and girl patterns from page 33 and 34. Enlarge copies of the star on page 36 and display student work on the stars. Give the board a finishing touch by adding fabric on each side for stage curtains. Use the top hat and cane patterns from page 35 to give your board a touch of "Broadway."

Additional Uses

- List "Star" classroom spellers.
- Use the bulletin board to announce or list performers in a play or talent show.
- Use copies of the star pattern to list jobs and student names for a "Star Helpers" job assignment board.
- Have students write about favorite movie/television stars and display on top hats.

Finishing Touches

- Make aluminum foil stars to use as a border.
- Use black contact paper or fabric for curtains.
- Attach colorful fabric to the bulletin board as a backdrop.
- Decorate the bulletin board with "star" attire, i.e., sunglasses, shiny fabrics, etc.
- Cut pictures of students' favorite movie stars from magazines to use as a background.

Creative Captions

- Presenting Good Work
- A Class Act
- All the World's a Stage
- Star Struck
- Great Work Deserves the Spotlight
- One Stage at a Time
- Setting the Stage for Good Work
- Great Performances
- Hats Off to Great Writing
- Topping Off the Year

Boy Pattern

34

35

WRAPPING UP GOOD WORK

Display students' best efforts on this "Wrapping Up Good Work" bulletin board. Use wrapping paper to decorate the bulletin board background as a present. Enlarge the balloon patterns on page 41 and place at the sides of the board. Enlarge several copies of the gift bag pattern on page 40 and display student work on them.

Additional Uses

- Use gift patterns as reward coupons.

- Write questions on gift boxes or bags and have students lift the gifts to reveal the answers.

- Have students list "gifts of themselves" that they can give to the community.

- List student birthdays on gift boxes and bags.

- Color the gifts to correspond with specific holidays (i.e., Christmas, Mother's Day, etc.).

Finishing Touches

- Use a big piece of butcher paper or ribbon to make a bow.

- Cover the gift pattern with wrapping paper.

- Attach real balloons to the board.

- Wrap empty boxes with decorative paper and bows and attach these to the bulletin board.

- Use wrapping paper as a border or background.

Creative Captions

- Gifted Work
- Wrapping Up Good Work
- Patterns of Gifts
- Gifts From the Heart
- Unwrap a Super Worker
- Shining Wrap
- A Bundle of Gifts
- Surprising Ideas
- Handle With Care
- Let's Have a Party
- It's Better to Give Than to Receive

Balloon Patterns

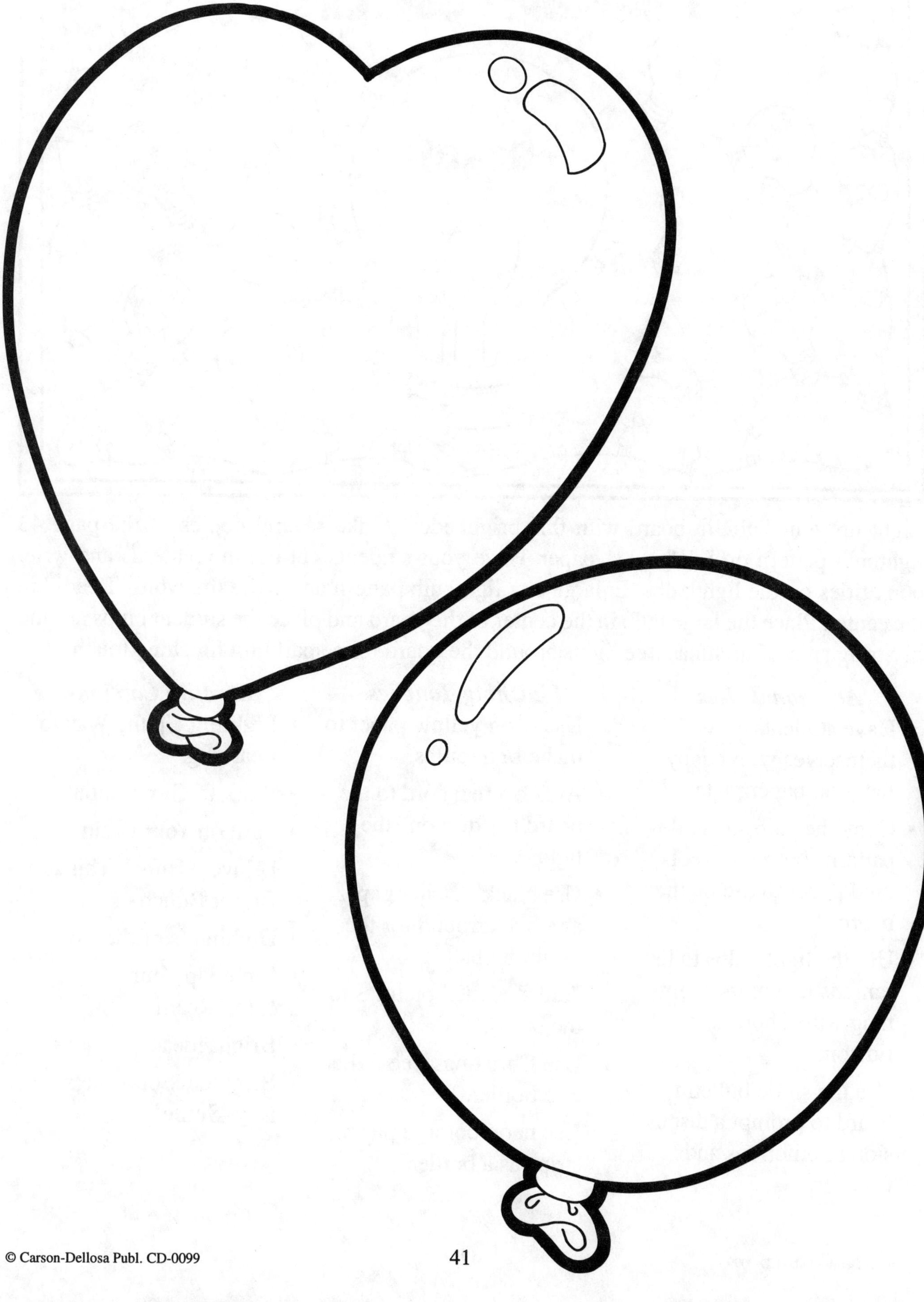

Light up your bulletin board with this bright idea. Make several copies of the page 43 lightbulb pattern on 8 ½" x 11" paper. Have your students cut out the patterns and write book titles on the lightbulbs. Enlarge one lightbulb pattern and write the word "Read!" in the center. Place the large bulb in the center of the board and place the student bulbs around it. String small Christmas tree lights around the board for a sparkling finishing touch.

Additional Uses

- Have students draw themselves with happy faces on paper plates.
- Copy the page 44 smile patterns onto neon-colored paper to use on the board.
- Use the light bulbs to list famous inventors beginning with Thomas Edison.
- Use the smile bulletin board to prompt a discussion of emotions and feelings.

Finishing Touches

- Use neon yellow paper to make light bulbs.
- Attach a real cord to the board to "turn on" the lights.
- Use black butcher paper as a background for the bright bulbs.
- Add students' pictures to the bulbs.
- Use Christmas tree lights as a border.
- Use neon-colored paper strips as a border.

Creative Captions

- Lighting Up the Way to Learning
- Work to Glow About
- Turn on Your Brain
- I Have a Hunch This is a Bright Bunch
- Highlights of the Book
- Light Up Your Life...Read!
- Bright Ideas
- Brighten Someone's Day–Smile!

Stir up your students' reading list with this bulletin board. Use the patterns on pages 46, 47 and 48 to create a yummy classroom display. Write book titles on the vegetable patterns and display them around the soup pot centerpiece. Don't forget to add some finishing touches like a checkered tablecloth for a background.

Additional Uses

- Have students bring in family recipes and write them on copies of the page 50 recipe card.
- List story titles on the vegetables.
- Have the students cut out pictures of healthy foods from magazines and glue these to the board.
- Use this board to display science experiments using celery and red dye.
- Use for a cooking class.

Finishing Touches

- Make a bright tissue paper fire under the pot.
- Attach a real chef's hat to the chef pattern on page 49.
- Decorate the board with real utensils.
- Use an apron for decoration.
- Make a background with a checkered tablecloth.
- Put students' pictures on recipe cards to display.
- Have the students bring in their own recipes to share.

Creative Captions

- Our Recipe for Cooperation
- Our Mixture for Success
- A Recipe for Friendship
- Cooking Up Good Workers
- Look What We've Cooked Up
- Cooking Our Way to the Food Pyramid
- Tasting Great Work
- Stir Up a Good Story
- Mixing Up a Great Class

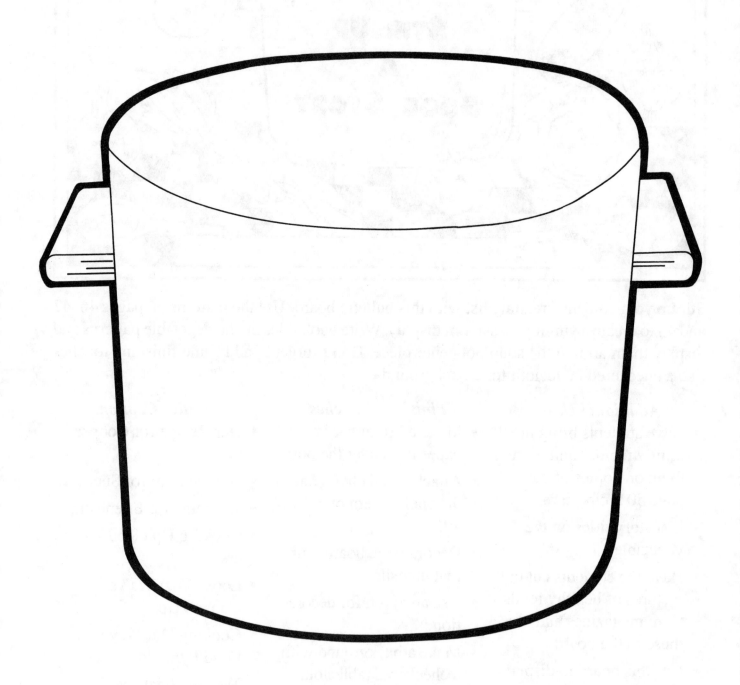

49

From the kitchen of…

Create a board of fun with this circus bulletin board. Reproduce the patterns on pages 52 and 53. Put each student's name and picture onto a balloon. Place balloons around the board and in the clown's hands. The circus tent, elephant, and peanut patterns on pages 54, 55 and 56 can also be utilized for a creative circus setting that is truly "under the big top!"

Additional Uses

- Have students draw their faces on paper balloon cutouts.

- Have the students cut out pictures of animals from magazines to add to the circus.

- Use paper plates to make clown faces. Use wallpaper, buttons, cotton, etc., for features.

- Use paper bags to create circus costumes for stuffed animals the students have brought from home.

Finishing Touches

- Use a piece of rope for a high wire.

- Attach a sheet to the board to make a big top tent.

- Use cotton balls for clown noses.

- Blow up balloons and tape to the bulletin board as a border.

- Glue real peanuts or peanut shells to the board.

Creative Captions

- "Clowning" Around
- Mr./Mrs. ____'s Circus
- Buckets of Fun
- Circus News
- Balance on the High Wire
- Three Rings of School
- Big Top Fun
- Circus Fun
- High Wire Math
- Funny Fantasy Stories
- Nuts About Science/Math
- Big Top Topics

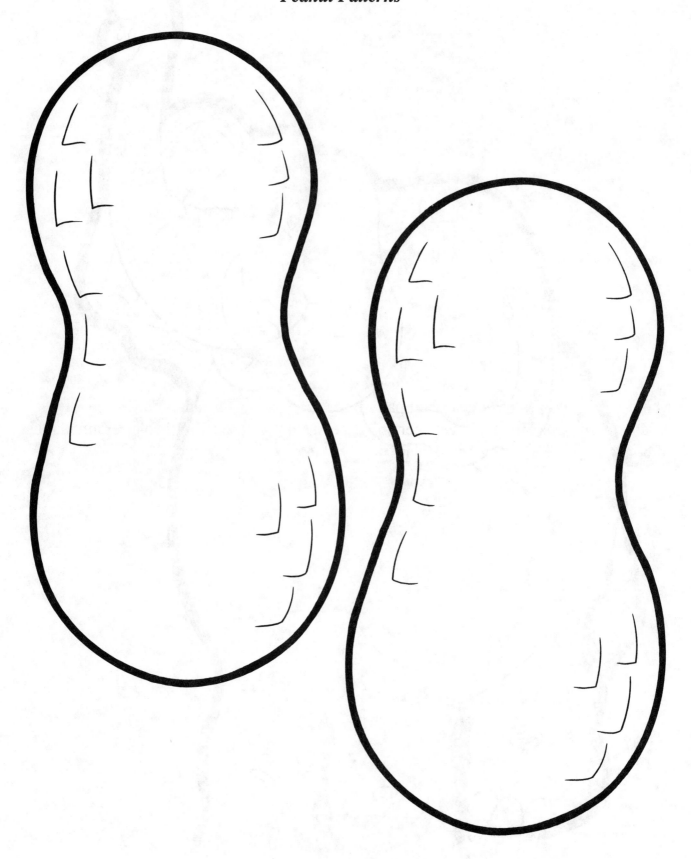

Hit a Reading Home Run

Be a hit with your students with this baseball bulletin board. Use the patterns on page 58. Make enough copies of the baseball pattern for every student's name. Each time a student reads a book, have him place a sticker on his personalized baseball. When a certain number of books are read by a student, declare that he has scored a home run!

Additional Uses

- Have students create baseball cards with themselves as the players. Display these on the bulletin board.
- Use copies of the mitt and ball to make a matching interactive bulletin board.
- List rules for good sportsmanship on the baseball equipment.
- Use the board as an area to graph students' favorite sports.
- Have your students design a baseball uniform.

Finishing Touches

- Use fringed construction paper to make grass.
- Hang real baseball hats on the bulletin board.
- Use sports wrapping paper as a background.
- Use sandpaper or dirt to create a realistic pitcher's mound.
- Use fabric to create uniforms for the page 60 and 61 girl and boy players.
- Use a brown shoelace to add stitches to the mitt.
- Use the cap and home base patterns on page 59 for art or writing.

Creative Captions

- On the Ball
- Have a Ball
- Winding Up a Winner
- Home Run Reader
- It Takes Teamwork
- You're a Hit With Me
- Our Winning Team
- Catching Great Ideas
- Out With Bad Manners
- Pitching in a New Year
- Slide into Math
- Fielding New Ideas
- Pitch In and Help a Classmate

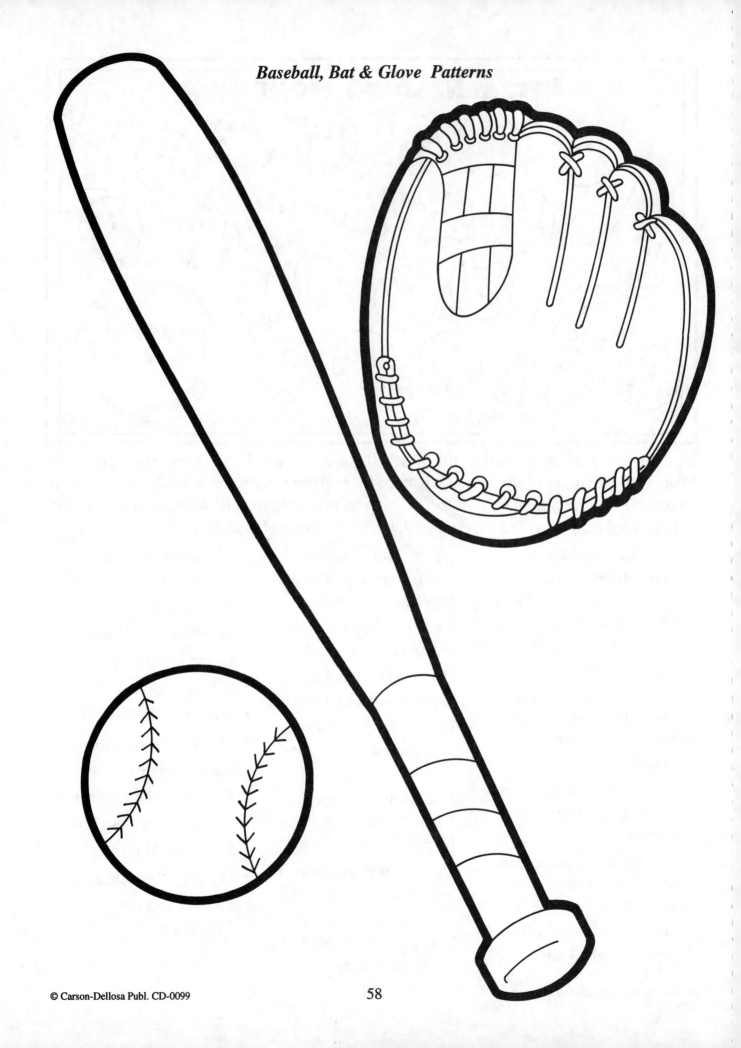

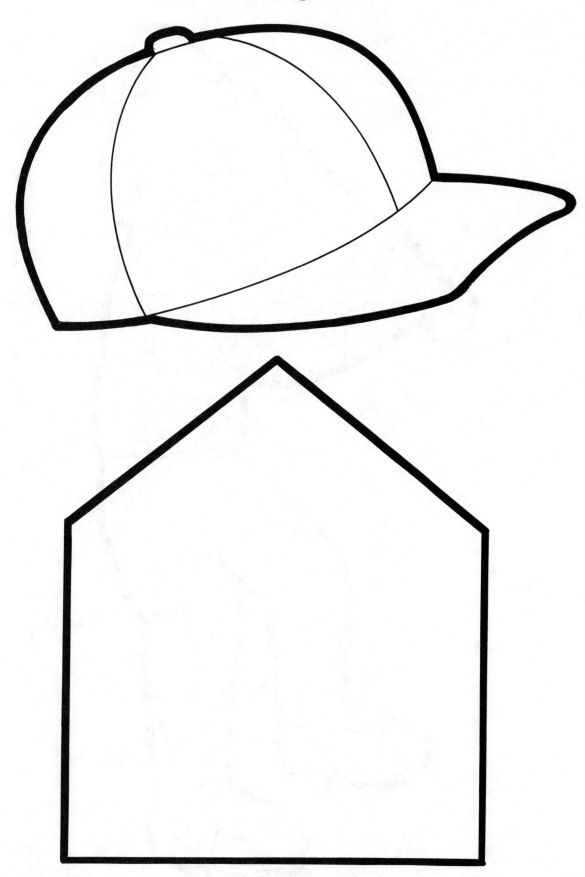

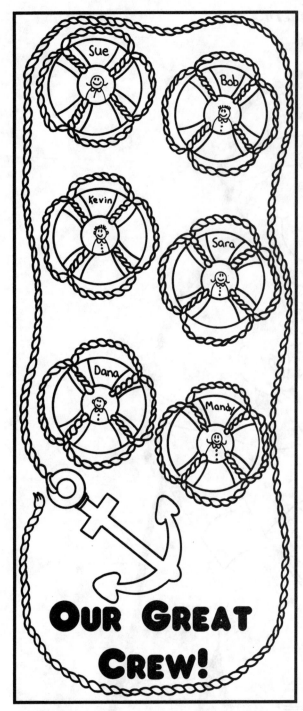

OUR GREAT CREW!

Welcome your crew aboard with this bulletin board! Enlarge and copy the patterns on page 64 and 65. Write each student's name on a life preserver. When students arrive, take their pictures with an instant camera and place the pictures inside the life preservers' holes. Use rope attached to the anchor as a decorative border.

Additional Uses

- Use the sailboat and anchor patterns as matching pieces for an interactive bulletin board.
- Graph the number of students who have been on a boat and the number of students who haven't been on a boat.
- Have students create a tourist/vacation guide using some of the patterns provided.
- Have students create treasure maps on brown butcher paper. Display the maps on the bulletin board.

Finishing Touches

- Use blue tissue paper or plastic wrap for the ocean.
- Attach a fish net to the board for a backdrop.
- Use a thick white rope for the border.
- Use a silver marker or aluminum foil to make an anchor.
- Have students make and decorate paper sailor hats. Showcase these on the board.
- Display colored copies of the page 66 and 67 patterns on the bulletin board. Place a bandana around the boy's neck and a scarf around the girl's neck.

Captions

- Sailing Toward Success
- Set Sail on a New School Year
- Fantastic Fleet
- Super Sailors
- Ships Ahoy
- Smooth Sailing
- Ship Shape
- Our Great Crew
- Sailing Toward a New Tomorrow

Sailboat Pattern

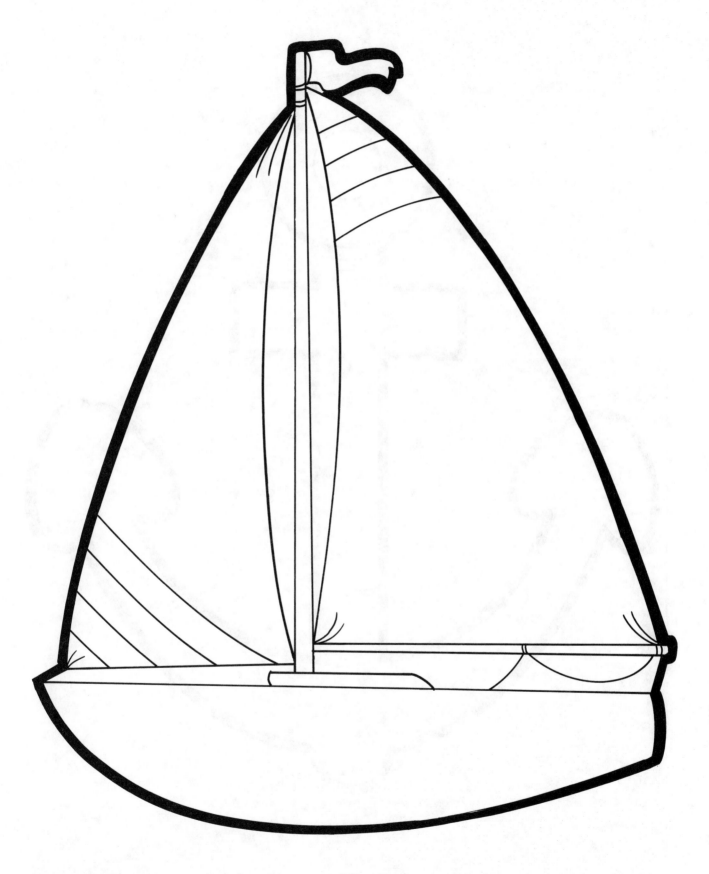

63

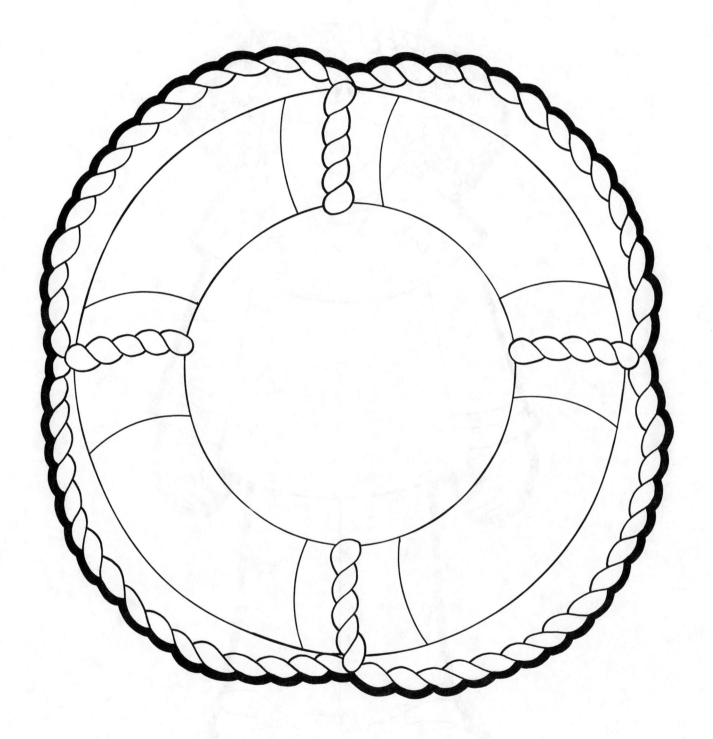

"SEA" OUR GREAT WORK

Display class work for all to "sea!" Use the patterns on pages 71 and 73 to decorate the perimeter of the board. Attach student work in the center. Scatter sea life around the work to complete the board.

Additional Uses

- Bring in a real aquarium for students to observe. They can use it as a model for the class bulletin board.

- Have students research the different types of sea life. Have them make their own creatures to place alongside the fish on the board.

- Compare the habitats of oceans, rivers and lakes. Show each habitat on the bulletin board.

- Use the fish and fish bowl patterns to create an interactive math manipulative game.

Finishing Touches

- Use fish net as a backdrop.

- Attach clear or blue plastic wrap over the scene for water.

- Use plastic plants to add greenery.

- Add blue tissue paper and shiny paper bubbles.

- Use painted pasta in different shapes for coral and shells.

- Use painted packing peanuts as coral, shells or sea life.

- Display colored copies of the page 69 and 70 Scuba Girl and Boy patterns.

Creative Captions

- "Sea" Our Great Work

- Swimming into Great Skills

- Hooked on Math

- Glad to "Sea" You

- Sea Star of the Week

- Swimming in a School

- School's Out for Summer

- Fishy Facts

- What a Catch!

- Catching Great Work

70

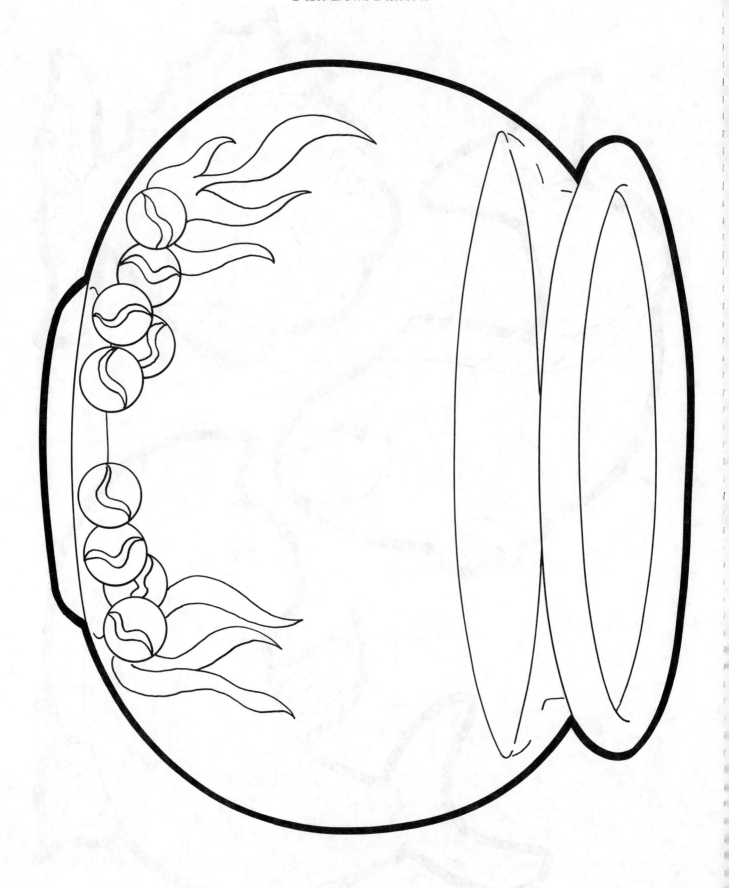

This bulletin board is a "blooming" good way to display student writing! Spring into action by enlarging the patterns on pages 75 and 76. Place flowers in each flowerpot, and display student writing on the front of each flowerpot. Copy the patterns on page 78 to add a springtime "buzz" to your board.

Additional Uses

- Put students' pictures in the centers of the enlarged flower patterns. Have classmates write descriptive words about each other on the petals.
- Use flowers and flowerpots as matching pieces for an interactive bulletin board.
- Use the bees' wings or the raindrop patterns to list spring vocabulary or spelling words.

Finishing Touches

- Use wrapping paper for a background.
- Make tissue paper leaves or flower petals.
- Use cellophane or foil to make shiny raindrops.
- Create grass out of fringed colored paper.
- Allow students to color the butterfly patterns with bright markers.
- Use dried flowers or potpourri as a border.
- Use watercolors on coffee filters to create flower heads.

Creative Captions

- Blooming With Pride
- Blooming Good Work, Mate
- Spring into Math
- April Showers Bring May Flowers
- Mr./Mrs. _____'s Budding Authors
- Budding Artists
- Showers and Flowers
- Planting a New Beginning
- May Sunshine Smile Upon You
- Growing New Skills

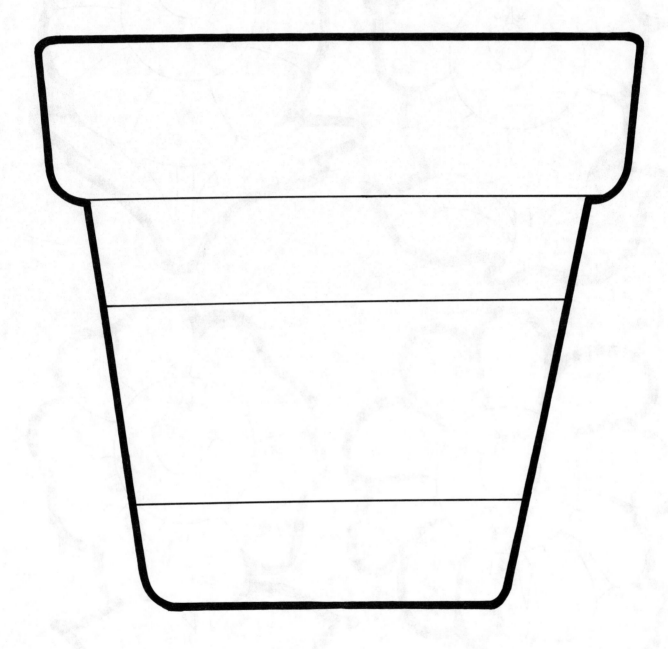

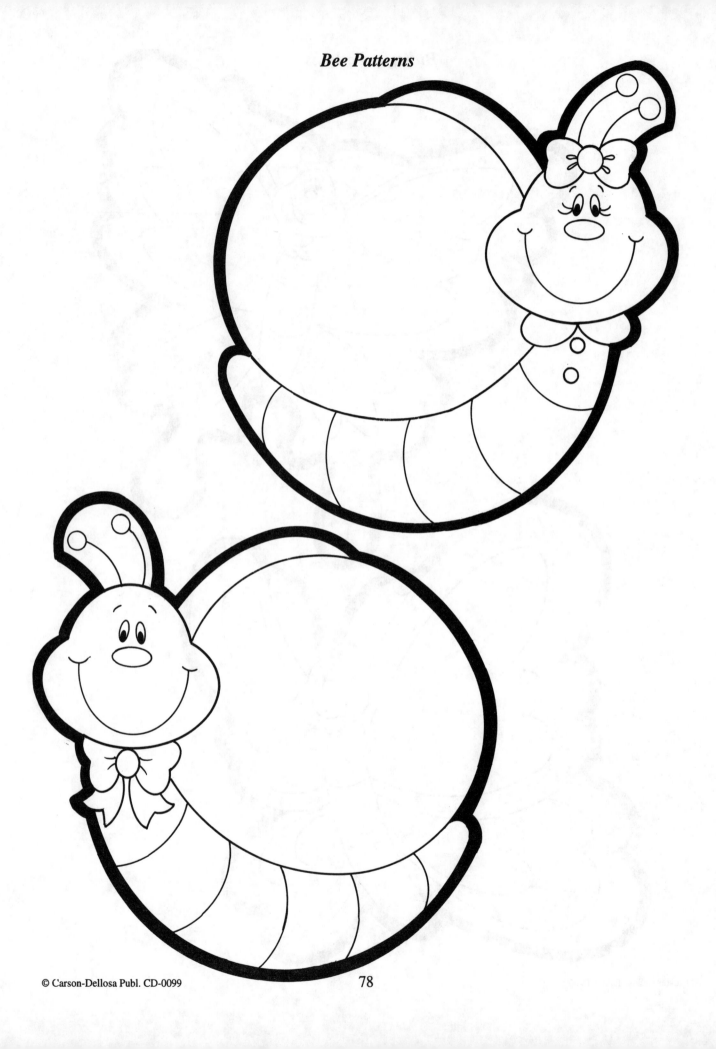

A RAINBOW OF GREAT WORK

Add a splash of color to your classroom with this rainbow bulletin board. Enlarge and color the rainbow and pot of gold patterns from pages 82 and 86. Place these on the board and display student work around them. Glue gold-wrapped chocolate coins around the board for a decorative (and delicious) border!

Additional Uses

- Have students bring in or wear clothing of a specific color one day each week.

- Study colors. Have students experiment with mixing fingerpaints on white paper. Display these under the rainbow.

- Use the pot of gold pattern on a St. Patrick's Day bulletin board.

- Use the page 84 and 85 boy and girl patterns on a Careers bulletin board.

Finishing Touches

- Use colored crayons, markers, paints, tissue paper and construction paper to decorate the board.

- Have students paint a rainbow on a white sheet to use as a background.

- Copy the page 83 sun pattern on yellow neon paper.

- Use a gold pen or gold foil to make extra gold coins.

- Use fabric in the colors of the rainbow to create a 3-dimensional rainbow.

Creative Captions

- A Rainbow of Excellence

- Books Take You Over the Rainbow

- We Are in a Colorful Class

- Our Class is Full of Color

- A Splash of Color

- A Rainbow of Great Work

- Our Treasure at the End of the Rainbow

- Follow the Rainbow to Success

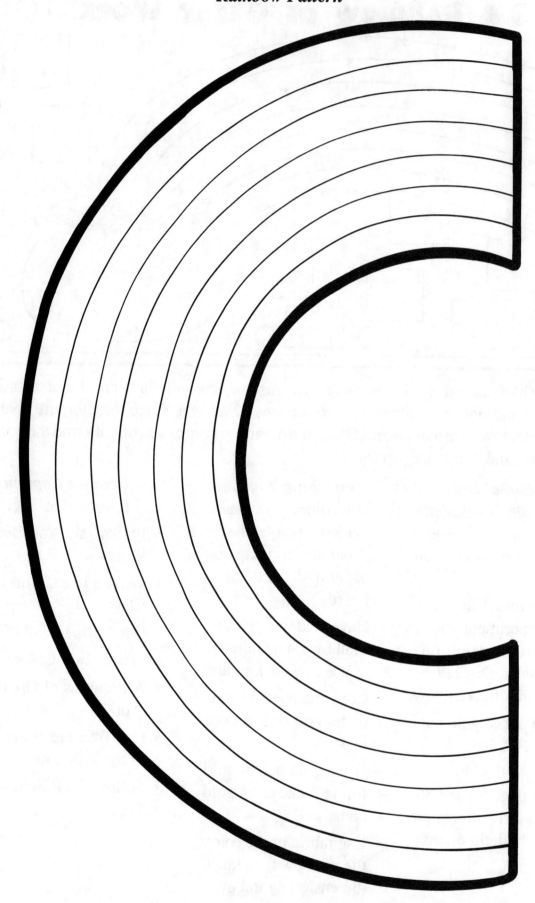

Open a door to reading with this bulletin board. Enlarge the patterns on pages 89 and 90. Place the reading worms on either side of the board. Place the bulletin board title on the pages of the open book. Staple book jackets on the board to create interest among your students!

Additional Uses

- Let students create book covers for their favorite books and mount these on the bulletin board.

- Graph students' favorite books on the board. Surround the graph with book jackets.

- Enlarge a page 88 bookmark pattern for each student and place it on the board. Have students place stickers on the bookmarks when they complete books.

Finishing Touches

- Use the patterns to record books students have read. Display these on the board.

- Have students design their own bookmarks to use as a border.

- Add ribbon or string to the tops of the bookmarks.

- Have students make their own bookworms using a variety of craft materials.

Creative Captions

- Spring Into Books
- Reading Stacks Up
- In My Book, You're A Great Class
- One for the Books
- A Pile of Good Readers
- Anything Can Happen When You Open a Book
- Open a World of Adventure – Read!
- Open a Book, Open Your Mind
- Mark This Class for Greatness

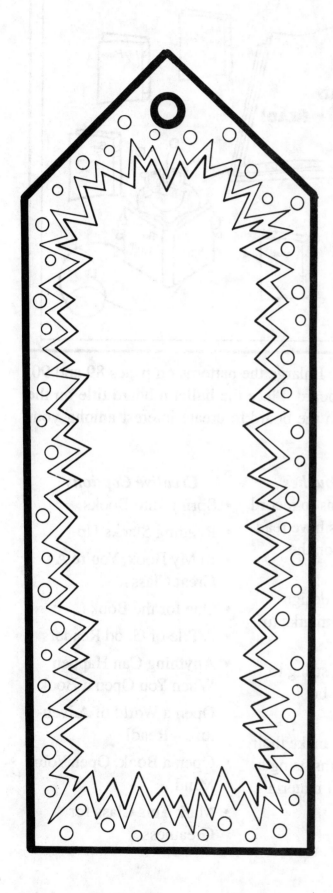

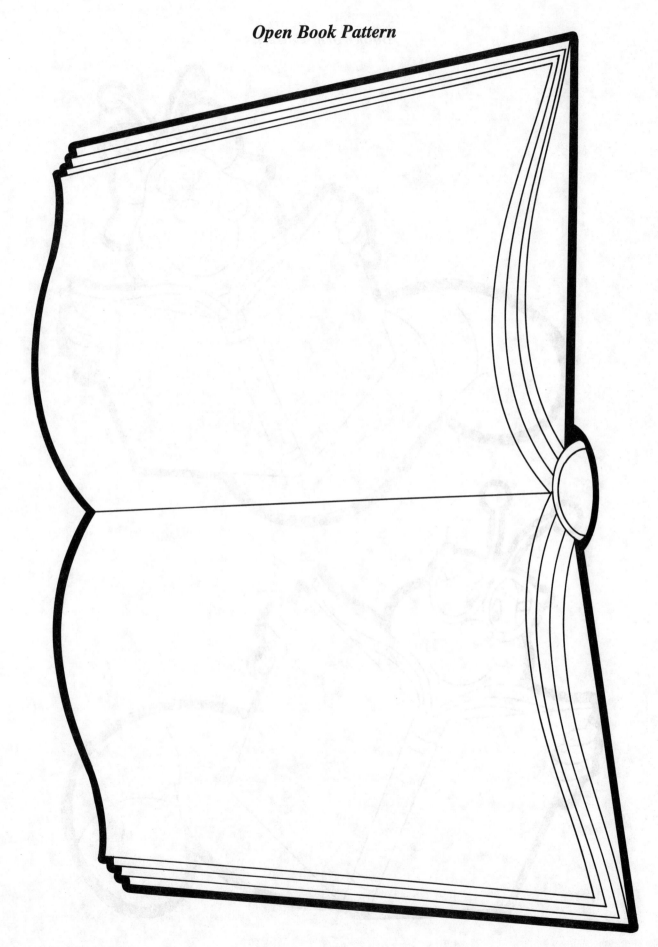

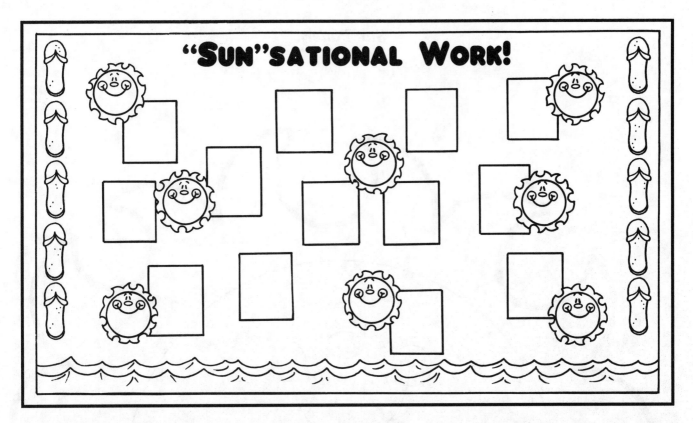

"Sun"sational Work!

Light up your classroom with this "Sunsational" bulletin board. Enlarge the pattern on page 92. Display student work beside or on top of the sun patterns. Add blue plastic wrap or butcher paper to the bottom of the board for water. Inexpensive flip-flop sandals make a super border. This is a great way to let your students' work shine!

Additional Uses

- Use the sun and cloud patterns as matching pieces for an interactive bulletin board.
- Graph the weather! Label a bar graph with *sunny, rainy* and *cloudy* days, and have students fill in the graph each day.
- Display students' pictures in the sun patterns for a "Shining Faces" bulletin board.
- Place the girl and boy patterns on the board and put students' summer stories around them.

Finishing Touches

- Use aluminum foil as a background or border.
- Use colorful tissue paper for the sun.
- Paint a rainbow on a sheet for the background.
- Use real sunglasses and empty sunscreen bottles for a border.
- Bring in summer outfits to decorate the bulletin board.
- Use flip-flop sandals as a border.

Creative Captions

- Shining Work
- Sunny News
- Bright Ideas
- Let Your Best Work Shine
- Eye Openers
- Step into Summer Reading
- Brilliant Students
- Blooming Good Ideas
- "Sun"sational
- Shining Examples

Summer Girl Pattern

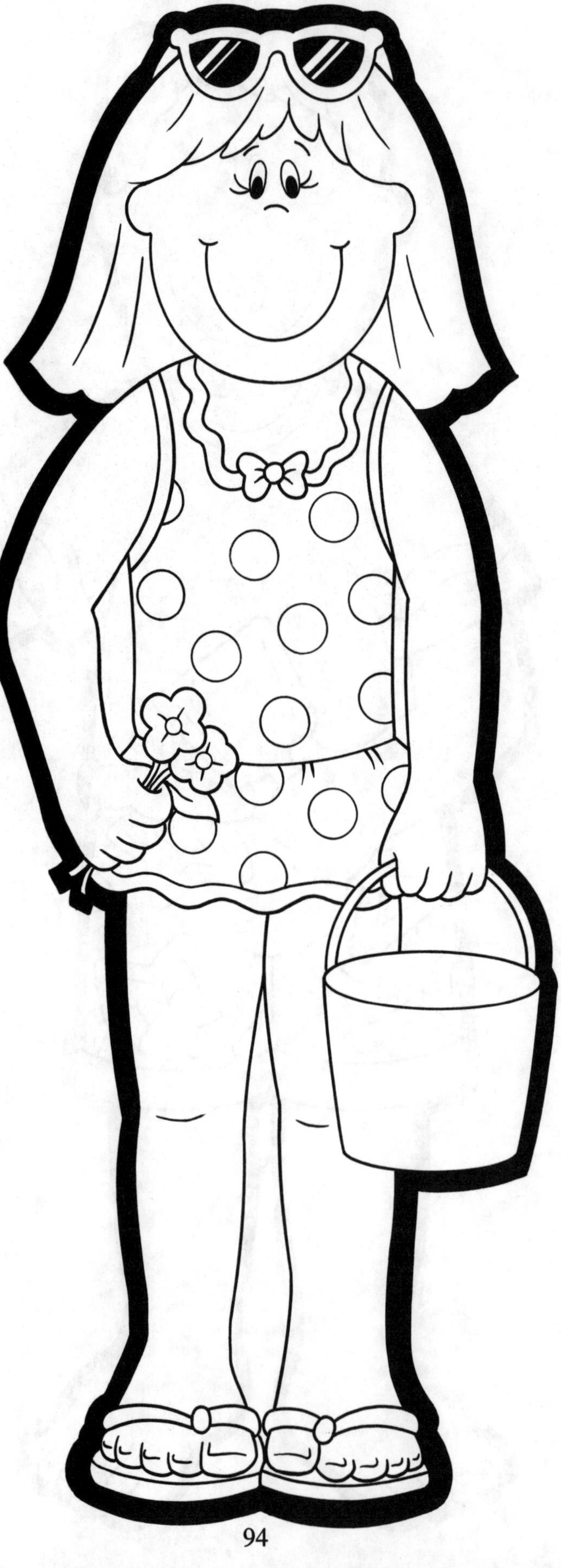

"BEARY" SPECIAL STUDENTS

What a "beary" cute bulletin board! Display copies of the bears and honey jar patterns from pages 97, 98 and 99 together on the board. Have students bring pictures of themselves to place on the honey jars.

Additional Uses

- Bring in a jar of honey and let students taste it.
- Read *Winnie-the-Pooh* by A.A. Milne (Dell, 1926) and list characteristics of Winnie on the bulletin board.
- Bring in a real hive for students to observe. Let them create a hive scene on the board using the page 78 bee and page 100 hive patterns.
- The bee and hive patterns may also be used as matching pieces for an interactive bulletin board.

Finishing Touches

- Use puffy paint or glue to make drops of honey.
- Put a real bow tie and hair bow on the bears.
- Use yellow felt to make honey for the hive.
- Make flowers out of cupcake liners.
- Use brown butcher paper to make a cave for the bears.
- Make clothes for the bears using fabric or wallpaper scraps.

Creative Captions

- "Beary" Good Work
- A Bear for All Seasons
- "Bear"ers of Good News
- "Bear" With Me
- Mr./Mrs. ___'s Honeybees
- Busy Bees
- "Beary" Special Students
- "Bee"utiful Days
- Mr./Mrs. ___'s Den
- "Honey" of a Job
- Have a "Beary" Good Day!

Swing into this great bulletin board using copies of the patterns on pages 102 and 104. Have students write their names on banana patterns. Use brown and green butcher paper to create trees. Place the bananas with student names on the trees. Display the monkeys below the trees.

Additional Uses

- Take a survey to find out how many students like bananas and make a graph of the results.

- Use the bulletin board to graph students' favorite fruits.

- Create a world map bulletin board and have students research and mark where bananas are grown.

- Display the monkey underneath the page 103 vine pattern. Have students research and list facts about monkeys on the board.

Finishing Touches

- Make grass out of construction paper.

- Make bananas out of yellow felt.

- Let students write recipes for banana splits. Hang these on the board.

- Use real vines as a border for your bulletin board.

- Hang a "bunch" of plastic bananas beside your bulletin board for a realistic effect.

- Use greenery from a craft store to add to the vine.

- Use brown felt to add fur to the monkey.

Creative Captions

- Monkeying Around
- Top Bananas
- "A"peeling Math Facts
- Swing into Poetry
- Hanging From a Limb
- Great Monkey Tales
- Monkey Business
- Have a Swinging Time at School
- Swing Into Science
- A Fruitful Bunch
- Go Bananas Over Math

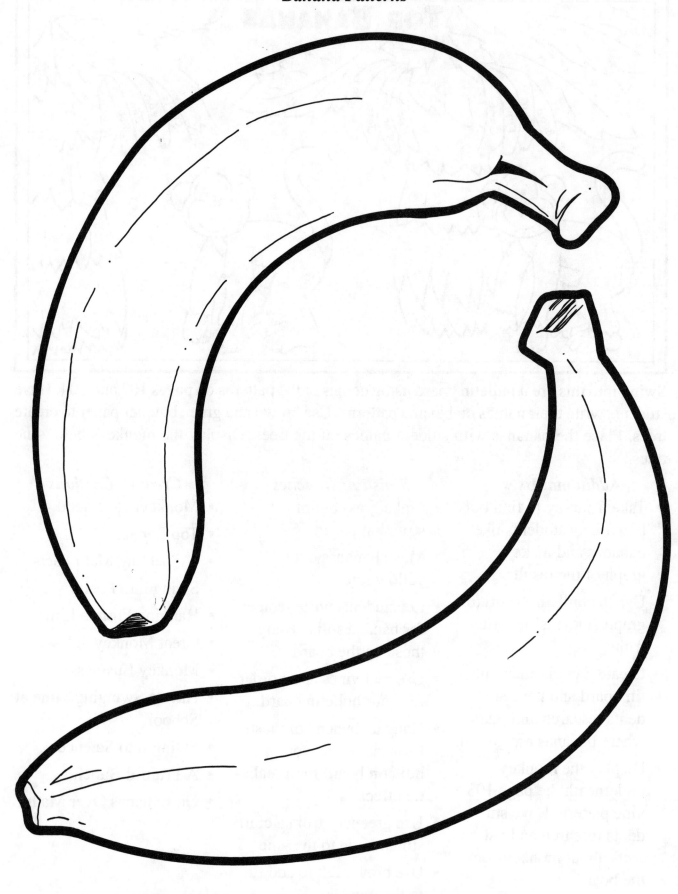

"Dog-Gone" Good Work

Bow-"Wow," what a great board to display student work! Use the patterns on pages 106, 107 and 108 to create a "dog-gone good" display. For a 3-dimensional effect, glue real dog bones to the board next to student work.

Additional Uses

- Use the board to graph students' favorite animals.

- Use the board as an incentive. List student names on the board. Each time a students completes a certain task, place a bone under his name.

- List jobs on doghouses and student names on dogs for a job assignment board.

- Compare and contrast different breeds of dogs on the board.

Finishing Touches

- Attach real dog bones to the board.

- Use a real dog collar or bandana on the dog's neck.

- Use sandpaper to cover the doghouse to make it more realistic.

- Use green construction paper to make a grass border.

- Use dog leashes or the page 109 dog bowl pattern as a border.

- Have students cut out pictures of dogs from magazines to use as a background or border.

Creative Captions

- Bow-"Wow"

- Hot Dog!

- Barking Up the Right Tree

- Howling Success

- Teacher's Pets

- "Ruffing" Up Good Work

- Bone Up on Your Math Skills

- We Are All Part of the Pack

- Dog-Gone Good Work

- Stay Out of the Doghouse

Bone Pattern

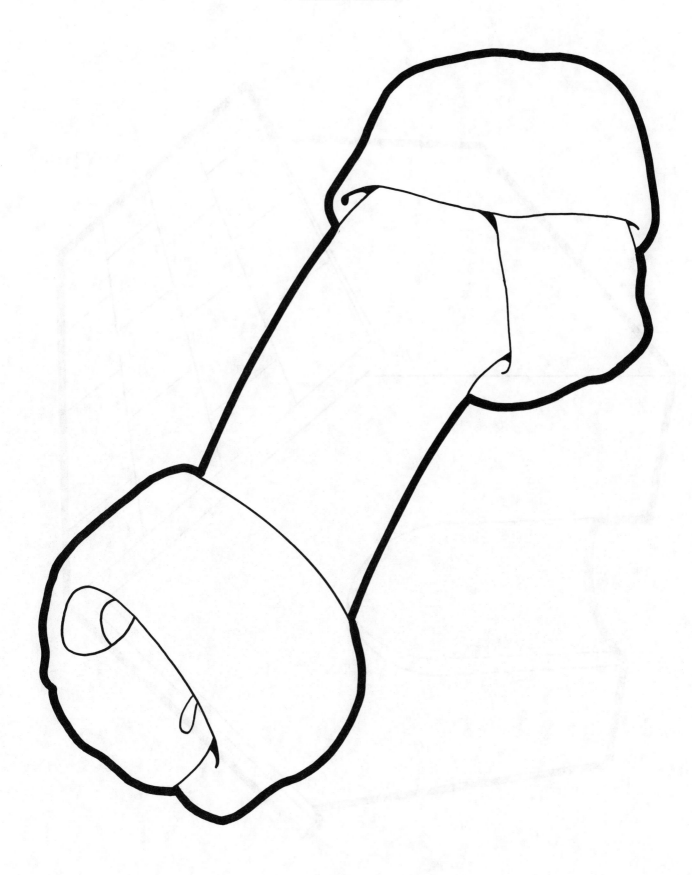

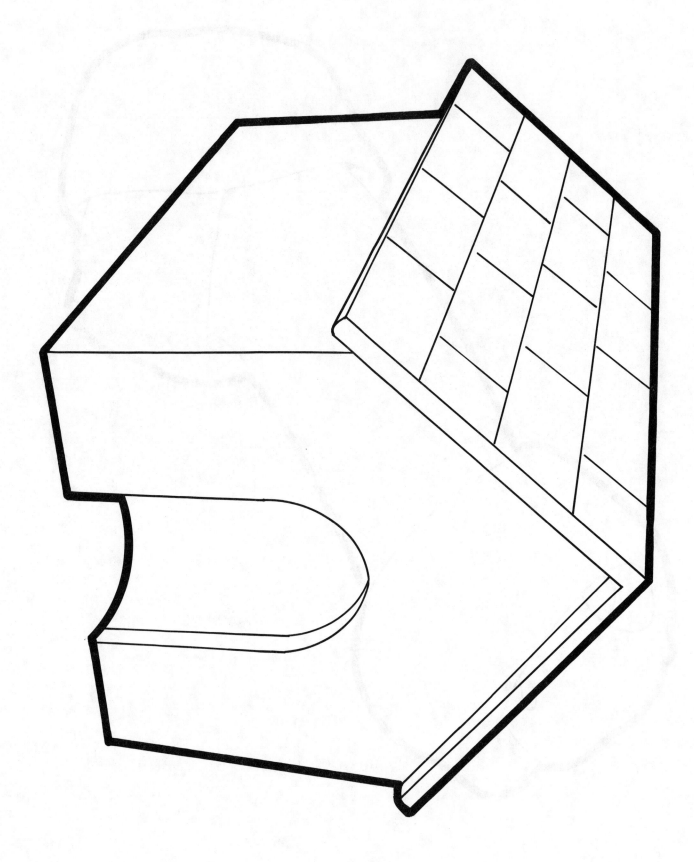

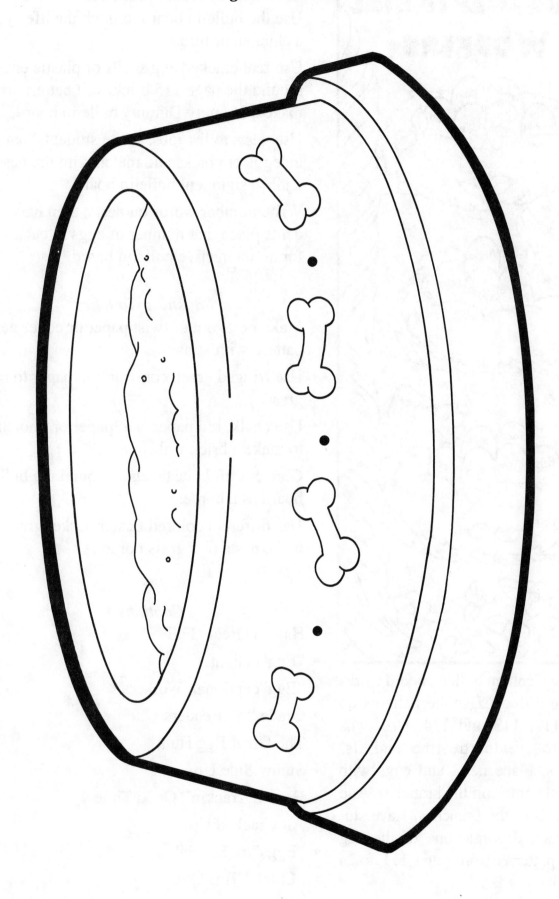

"EGG"CEPTIONAL WORKERS

This "egg"cellent bulletin board works great on a door! Use the patterns on pages 112, 113 and 114. Use twist paper to create the tree and its' branches. Place nests and eggs with students' names on the branches. Add baby birds to the branches. Have students each decorate one of the egg people patterns from page 111 for a decorative border.

Additional Uses

- Use the bulletin board to track the life cycle of a chicken or bird.
- Use real cracked egg shells or plastic eggs around the page 115 brick wall pattern to make a Humpty Dumpty bulletin board.
- Use nests to list jobs. Write students' names on eggs or chicks and match with the nests as a job assignment bulletin board.
- Write number words on nests, then have students place that number of eggs in each nest for an interactive bulletin board.

Finishing Touches

- Make nests out of twist paper or cover nest pattern with straw.
- Use fringed green construction paper to make grass.
- Use chalk, red paper, wallpaper or linoleum to make a brick wall.
- Glue colorful plastic eggs around the bulletin board as a border.
- Use different colored Easter basket grass to make nests or a grass border.

Captions

- Have a Great "Fall"
- "Egg"cellent
- "Egg"ceptional Workers
- Grade "A" Readers
- The Great Egg Hunt
- Sunny Side Up
- Have a Crackin' Good Time
- All Cracked Up
- "Eggs"tra Special
- "Chick" This Out

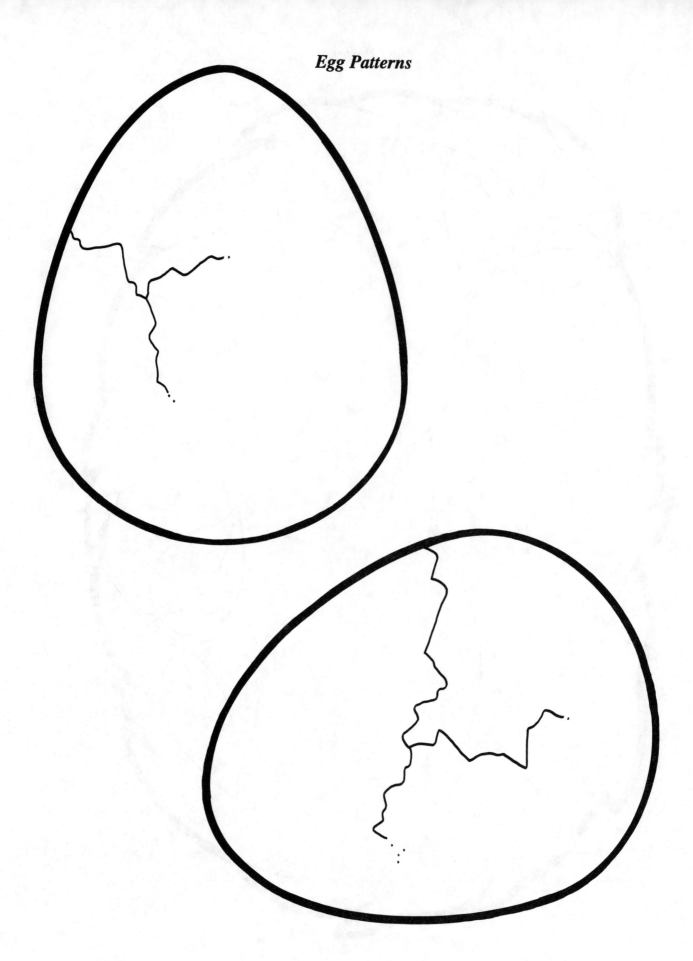

JUMP INTO READING

Charlotte's Web

The Happy Prince

Millions of Cats

Jump, Frog, Jump!

Jamberry

Frederick

Jump into a "toad"ally awesome classroom with this bulletin board. Use the patterns on pages 118, 119 and 120 to create a pond scene on your bulletin board. Add lily pads with book titles written on them. You may wish to add tissue paper flowers to the lily pads, or cover the board with plastic wrap for a "wet" effect.

Additional Uses

- Use the board to present the life cycle of a frog. Bring in a tadpole and allow students to document the transformation.
- Use the page 117 frog pattern and lily pads as matching pieces for an interactive bulletin board.
- Use the lily pads to list interesting facts about a pond habitat.
- Write jobs on leaping frog patterns. Write students' names on cattails and show the frog leaping over each set of names.

Finishing Touches

- Make lily pads out of felt, and flowers out of tissue paper.
- Provide paints for students to color frogs.
- Use party blowers for frog and toad tongues.
- Use blue or clear plastic wrap to create water around lily pads.
- Provide blue or brown butcher paper for students to create a swamp background.

Creative Captions

- Leaping Over Good Work
- Reading is "Toad"ally Awesome
- Think Green
- Jump Into Reading
- Leap Into a Good Book
- "Toad"ally Awesome Art Work
- Hop Into School
- Jump for a New Year
- "Frog"tastic Work
- I Am So "Hoppy" You Are Here

Leaping Frog Pattern

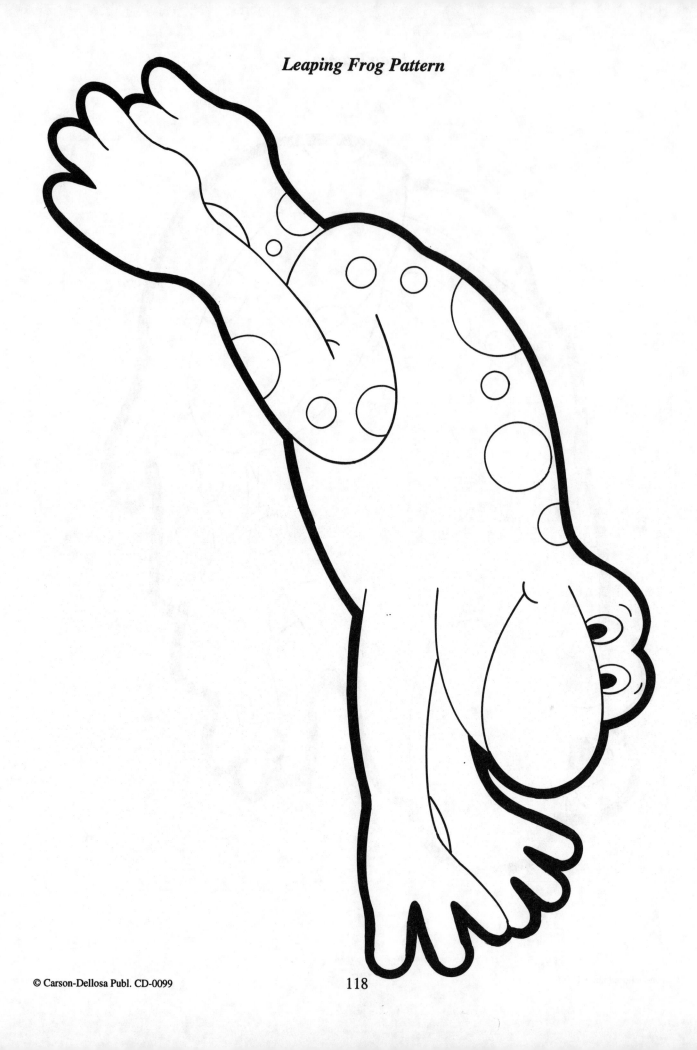

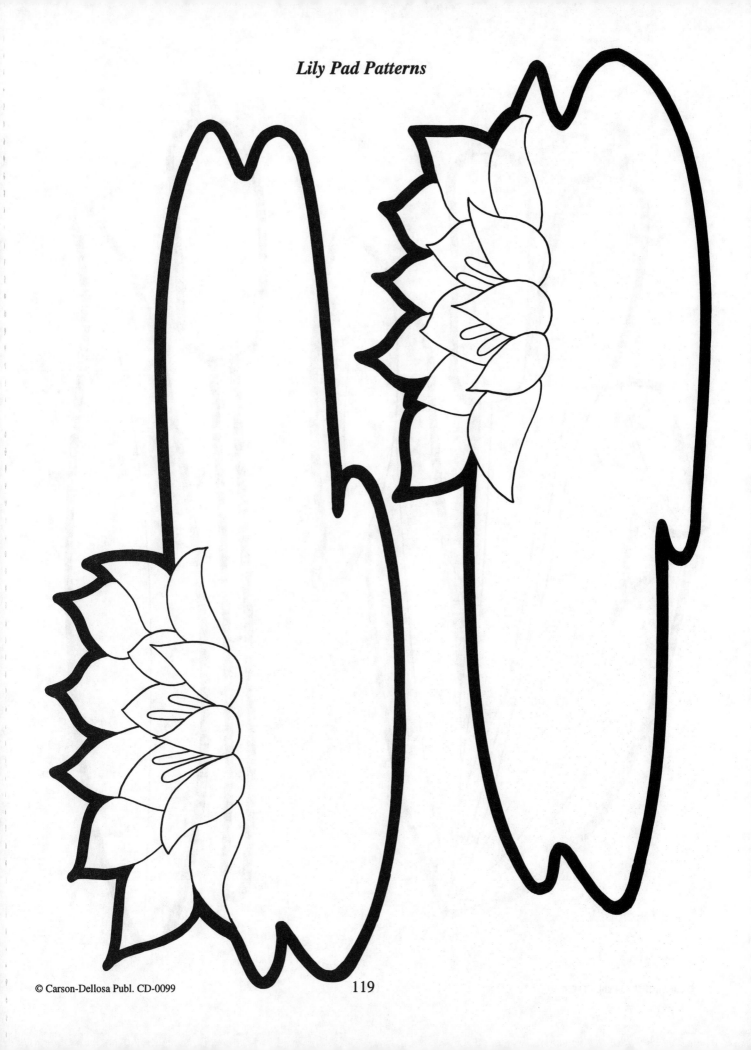

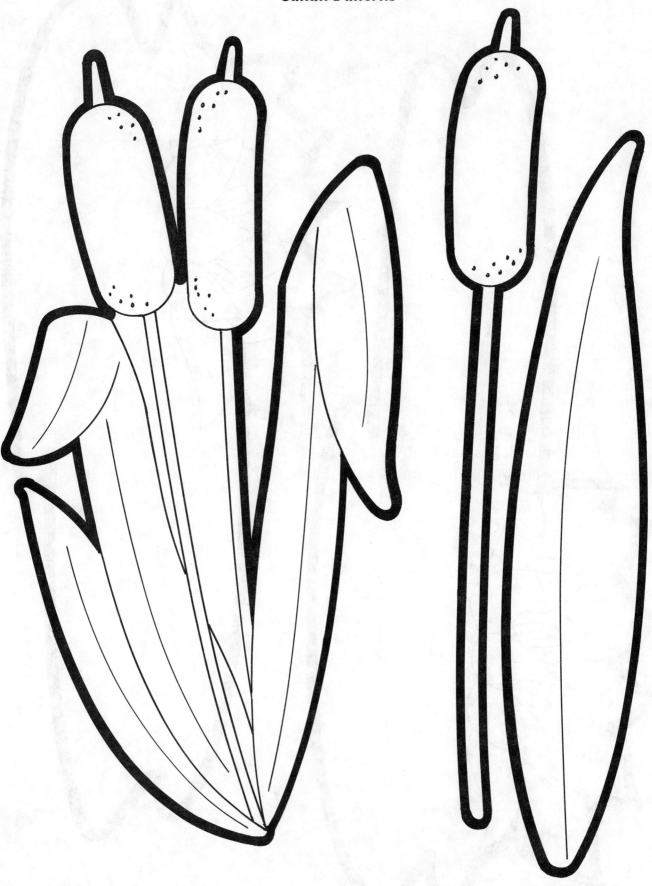

Have your students show their pride by displaying their work on this bulletin board! Enlarge the patterns on pages 122 and/or 123. Place one or both of these in the bottom corner(s) of the board. Display each student's work under a paw print pattern from page 124. Finish the board by adding yarn for the lions' manes, and green paper for grass.

Additional Uses

- Make a patterning game using paw prints and crowns.
- Create a world map bulletin board and have students research and mark areas where lions are found.
- Give each student a crown pattern and allow him to decorate with various art supplies. Display these on a "Crowning in a Smart Bunch" bulletin board.

Finishing Touches

- Use yarn for the lion's mane.
- Use gold foil or lamé for the crown.
- Make grass from green tissue paper.
- Curl brown paper to make lions' manes.
- Use glitter or paint pens to decorate the crown.
- Use craft fur to make a border.
- Have students paint paw prints on adding machine tape to use as a border.

Creative Captions

- Something to Roar About
- Lionhearted
- Pride in Good Work
- King of the Mathematics Jungle
- Royal Workers
- Roaring in a New School Year
- Pawing Our Way to Success
- Roaring About a New Class
- Crowning in a Smart Bunch
- Work Worth Roaring About

HARD WORK PAYS OFF

Let students' hard work pay off by displaying it on this bulletin board. Use the pattern on page 127 as a centerpiece. Display student work around the piggy bank pattern "filled" with coin patterns from page 129. Use additional coin patterns to accent each student's work. If desired, cover the pig body with pink felt before adding coins.

Additional Uses

- Copy a pig pattern for each student. Use as individual incentive charts with coin patterns as markers.

- Fill a jar with pennies and have students record their estimates on the bulletin board.

- Have students graph favorite farm animals on the board.

- Create an underwater scene on the board and add the page 128 treasure chest pattern with student names written on coins.

Finishing Touches

- Use a strip of rawhide leather for the pig tail.

- Add costume jewelry to the treasure chest.

- Write with a gold or silver paint pen.

- Use aluminum foil or foil wrapping paper for coins.

- Use pink felt to make a piggy bank.

- Use play money as a border or background.

- Make a treasure chest out of a cardboard box and allow students to decorate it with plastic "jewels."

Creative Captions

- Reading Makes Good "Cents"

- This Little Piggy Went to...

- Hard Work Pays Off

- Rich in Learning

- Priceless Work

- Worth Its Weight in Gold

- Knowledge is Cash in Hand

- Pig Out on a Good Book

- "Oink" for Math

- Our Class is a Treasure

- We Treasure Good Books

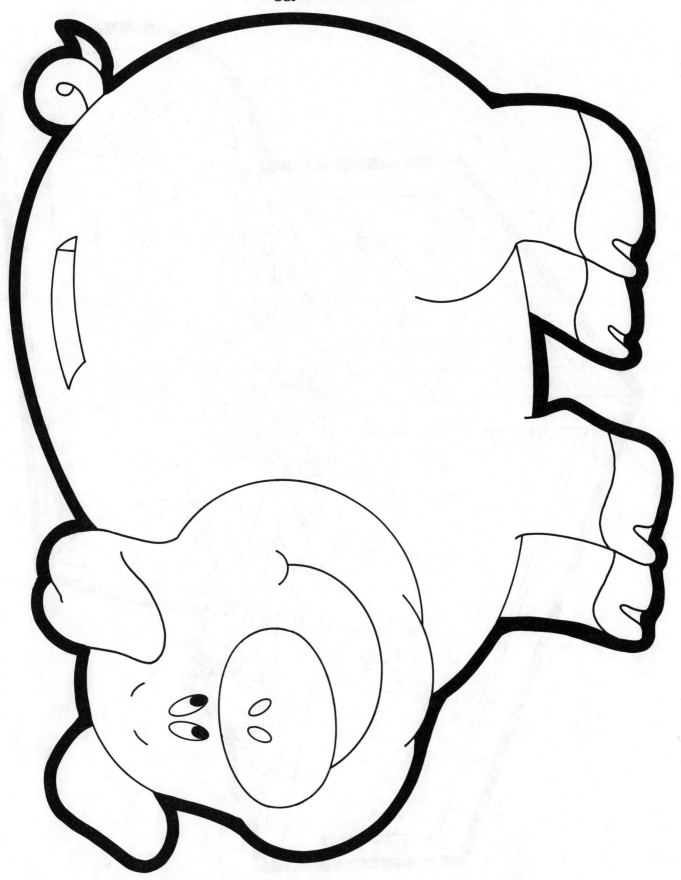

127

130

LOOK "WHOO'S" DOING GREAT WORK

Everyone will ask, "Whoo's Great Bulletin Board?" when you display these patterns in your room. Enlarge the patterns on page 132 to cover half of the board. Show the owl perched on the branch. Display student work around the owl and branch. For a finishing touch, use real leaves to accent student pages.

Additional Uses

- Write jobs on branches and students's names on owls. Place the owls on the correct branches to assign jobs.

- Display students' work under an enlarged page 134 eyeglasses pattern for a "See Our Great Work!" board.

- Discuss nocturnal animals. Display the owl and other animal shapes on a bulletin board with a dark blue background.

Finishing Touches

- Use butcher paper to create a forest backdrop.

- Use twist paper to create a three-dimensional branch.

- Use real feathers to decorate the owl or as a border.

- Add real leaves to the branch.

- Use neon yellow paper for the owl eyes.

- Use artificial greenery to decorate the branch.

Creative Captions

- Look Whoo's Doing Great Work

- Wise Owls

- Mr./Mrs. ___'s Wise Owls

- Sharp as an Owl

- Whooose Work Is This?

- Wise Birds Give a Hoot

- Give a Hoot

- Look Whoo's Landed in Our Class

- Whooo's So Smart?

- Whooo's a Good Worker?

- Wise Old Bunch

Reach "great heights" with this classroom bulletin board. Enlarge a kite pattern from page 136 for each student. Let students decorate their kites, then choose a piece of their work to display on the kite. Place the kites on a board titled "High-Flying Work." Let students add clouds and a sun to complete the board.

Additional Uses

- Discuss the history of flight and, using the patterns and a timeline, record the first flights of kites, hot-air balloons, planes and rockets.

- Provide various craft materials for students to make their own flight machines. Display these on a "Flying High" bulletin board.

- Duplicate several hot-air balloon patterns. List jobs on the balloons and students' names on cards which can be placed under the balloons.

Finishing Touches

- Use string or yarn for the balloon and kite strings.

- Tie real bows on kite tails.

- Use sky blue butcher paper for the background.

- Use cotton for clouds.

- Make a yellow sun out of butcher paper.

- Use green tissue paper for grass.

- Let students cover their kite patterns with colored tissue paper.

Creative Captions

- High-Flying Work
- Great Heights
- Flying High With Math
- Soaring High
- High-Lights
- Countdown to Success
- Spring is in the Air
- Burst into a New Tomorrow
- Look Who's Landed in Our Room
- Fly With Reading
- Soar to New Heights
- Moving Up

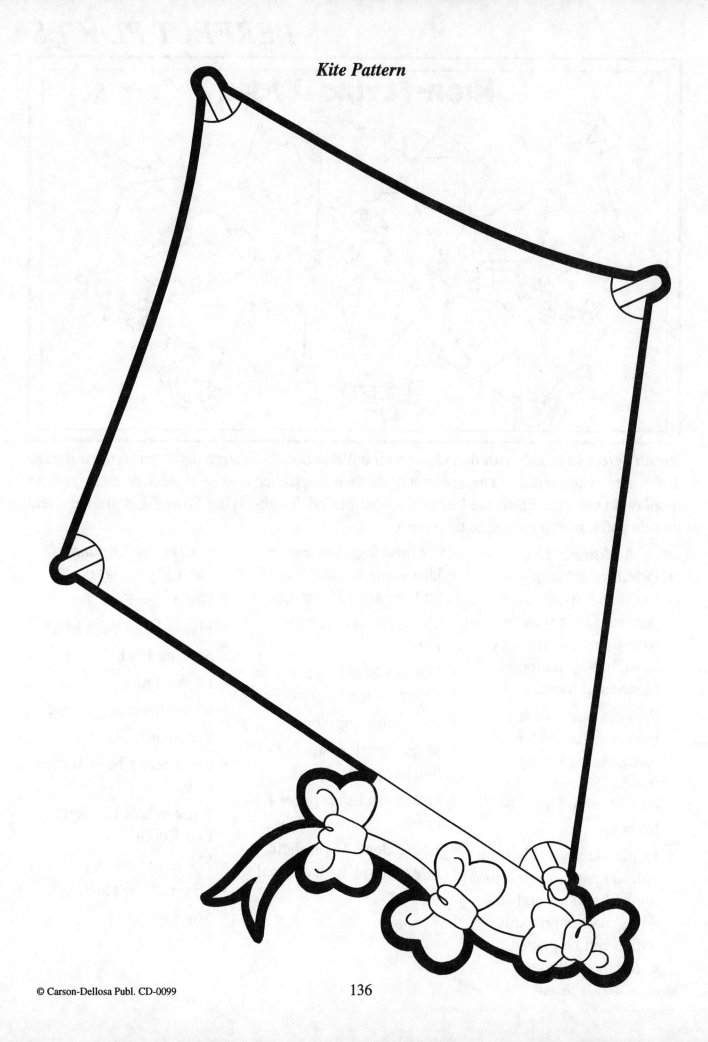

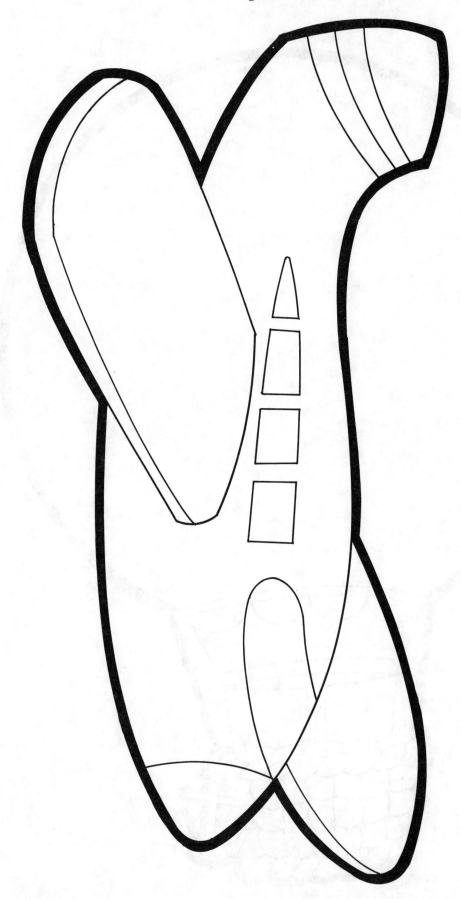

Rocket Pattern

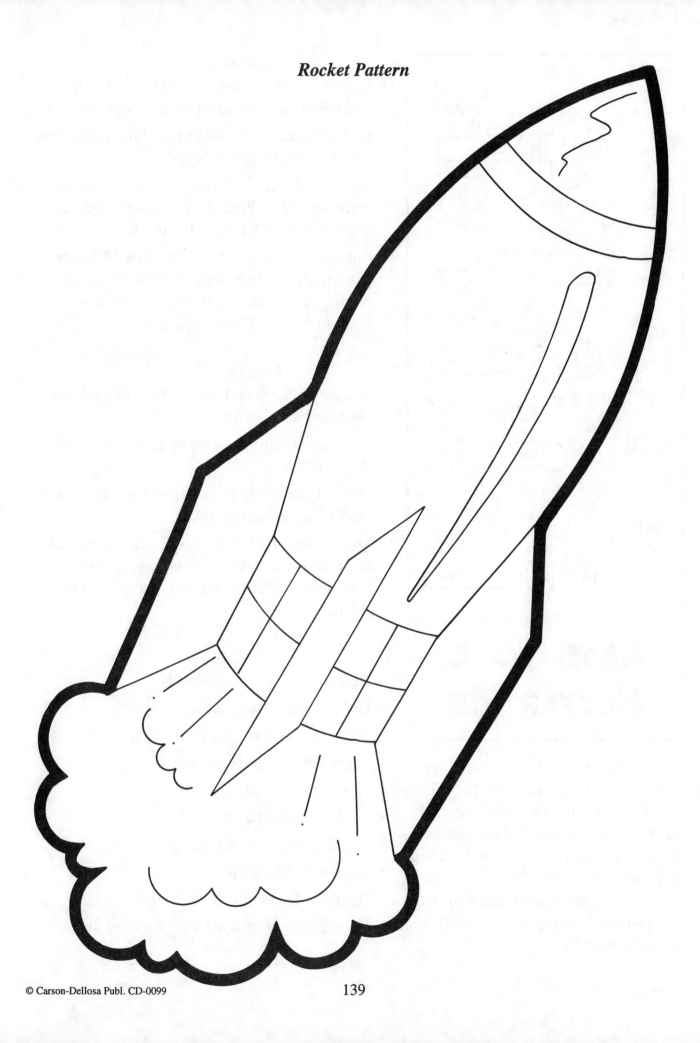

139

KEYS TO A BETTER ME

Good Manners are the "key" to a great year! Copy a pattern from page 141 for each student. Have students write their names along with good manners on the keys and display them on the classroom door for all to see! Use a sheet of butcher paper decorated with key prints (keys dipped in paint) for the background.

Additional Uses

- Provide a white sheet in the shape of a door and allow students to paint an adventure on it.
- Use keys and padlocks as matching pieces for an interactive bulletin board.
- Write book titles on padlocks. Write student names on keys. Place a key under a padlock when a student has read the book.
- Enlarge several copies of the page 142 door pattern. Place student pictures in the squares on the doors. Display these on an "Open the Door to a Great Class" board.

Finishing Touches

- Gather old keys and attach them to the bulletin board as a border.
- Use aluminum foil to make keys, locks and door knobs.
- Have students dip keys in paint and make key prints for the background.
- Display several types of padlocks in front of the board (i.e., combination, key, number) and allow students time to practice opening them.

Captions

- Reading Unlocks the World
- Unlock the Door to Adventure
- Turn the Key to Open Your Mind
- Open Yourself to New Ideas
- "Key" in on Math Skills
- Lock Out Bad Habits
- Six Keys to Good Skills
- Keys to a Better Me
- Open the Door to a Great Class!
- Good Study Habits are the "Key" to Success

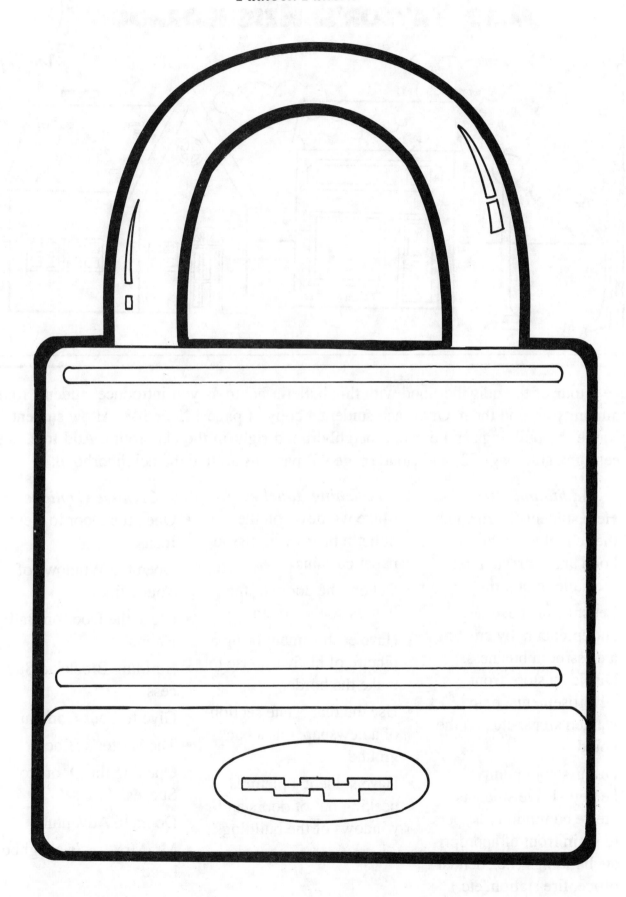

143

MISS TAYLOR'S NEIGHBORHOOD

Take a tour of the neighborhood with this bulletin board as you introduce students to the community around them. Give each student a copy of page 145 or 148. Allow students to decorate the buildings and create a neighborhood right in the classroom. Add tree, sign, street light, sun (page 92) and cloud (page 95) patterns around the neighborhood.

Additional Uses

- Help students learn about the school's neighborhood and recreate it on the bulletin board.

- Let students become entrepreneurs by creating a classroom business. Display a store front, advertisements, help wanted signs, etc., on the board.

- Discuss community helpers. Have students create community helpers to go in front of appropriate buildings (i.e., dentist office, fire station, etc.).

Finishing Touches

- Make windows on the bulletin board with tissue paper curtains.

- Cut out the doors of the houses so they open.

- Have each student bring a picture of his/her house to make the border.

- Use the real estate section of a newspaper as a background.

- Have student's pictures peeking out of doors and windows of the buildings.

Creative Captions

- Open the Door to New Ideas

- Open the Windows of Your Mind

- Close the Door on Bad Habits

- Building Blocks to Success

- Give to Your Community

- The Writer's Block

- Opening the Doors to Success

- Doors to Adventure

- Mr./Mrs. ___'s Neighborhood

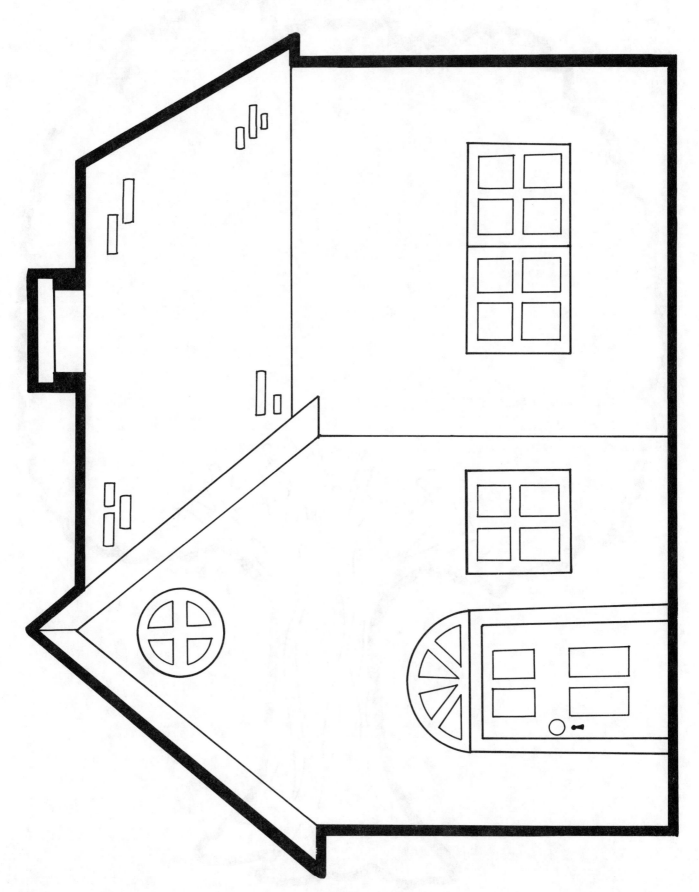

Street Light and Sign Patterns

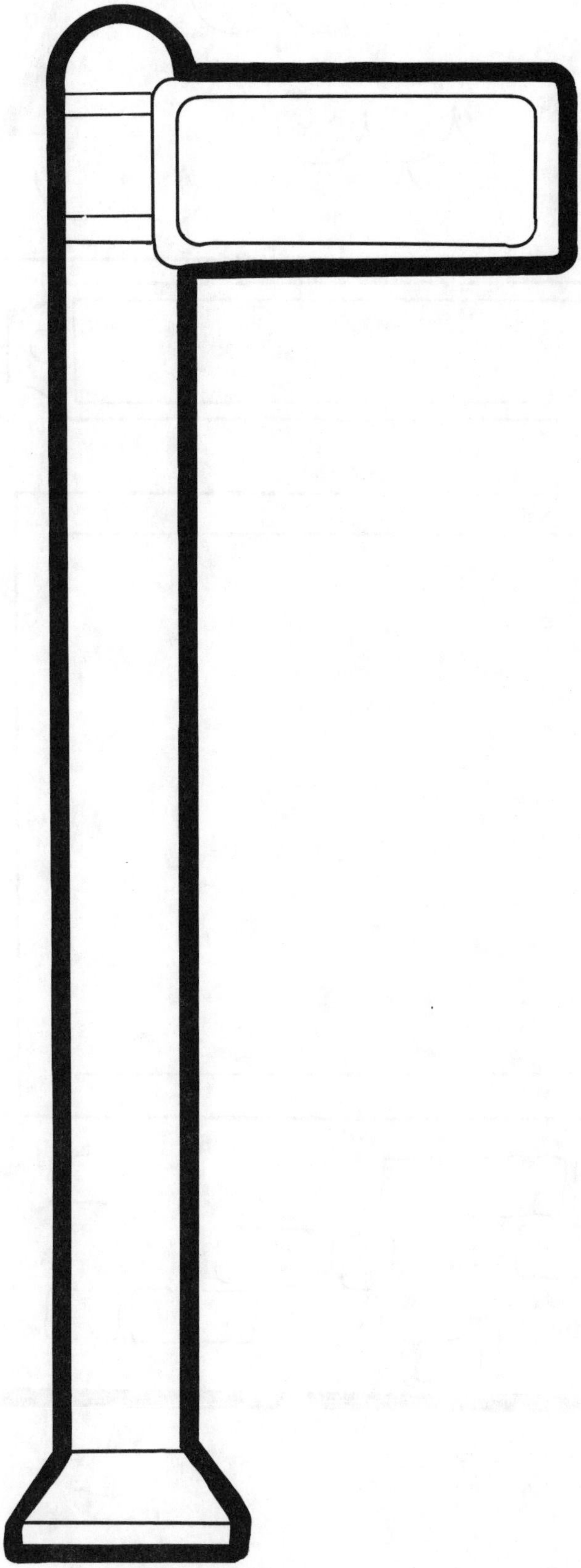

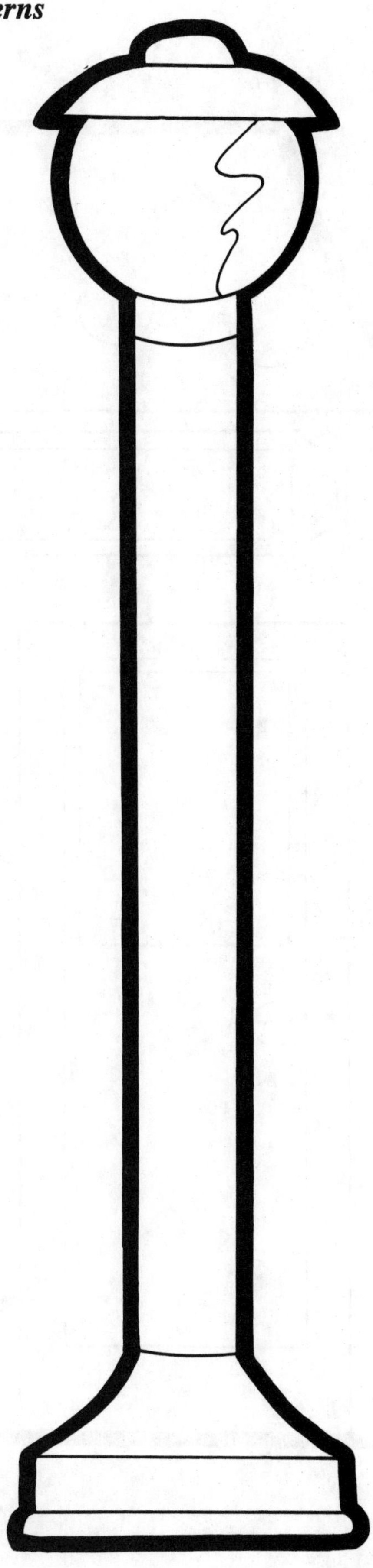

ALL ABOARD FOR LEARNING FUN!

Your students will "get on board" this learning train by displaying their best work! Copy and color the patterns on pages 150-153. Create a track across the bottom of your board with aluminum foil and attach the train to the track. Display student work above the train. To create a 3-dimensional effect, use cotton for the smoke!

Additional Uses

- Write the alphabet on train car patterns and display around the classroom.
- Use the engine and caboose patterns as matching pieces for an interactive bulletin board.
- Give each student a box car pattern and allow him to decorate it as he wishes. Display these attached to the engine pattern.

Finishing Touches

- Use aluminum foil to make railroad tracks and wheels.
- Use balsa wood as railroad tracks.
- Let students make box car sides with corrugated cardboard.
- Mount model train track around the bulletin board as a border.
- Copy and color the conductor pattern on page 154. Tie a real bandana around his neck.

Creative Captions

- We're on the Right Track
- All Aboard for Learning Fun
- Get Out of the Station and Into a Book
- Reading Railroad
- Conducting a Great Class
- Whistle-Blowing Math
- Roaring Ahead With Great Ideas
- Follow the Track to Success
- Non-Stop Learning
- A Load of Good Work

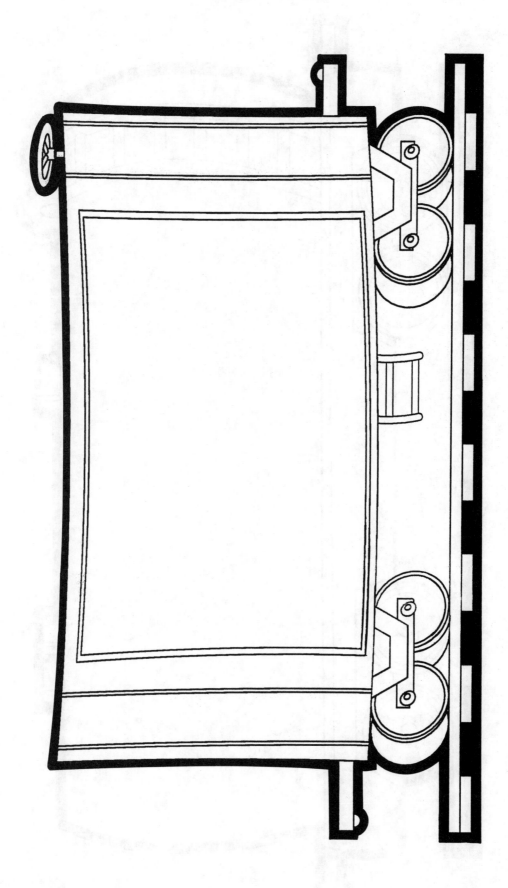

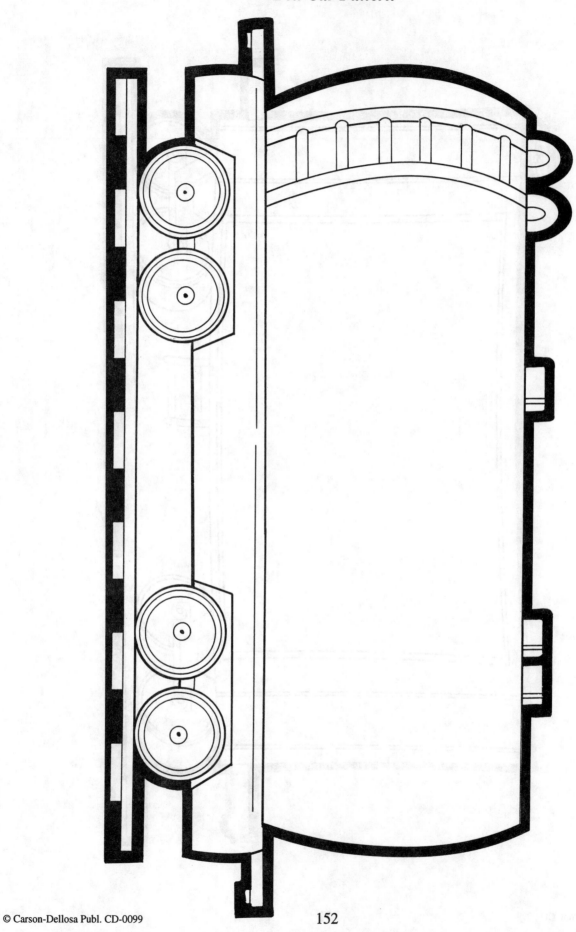

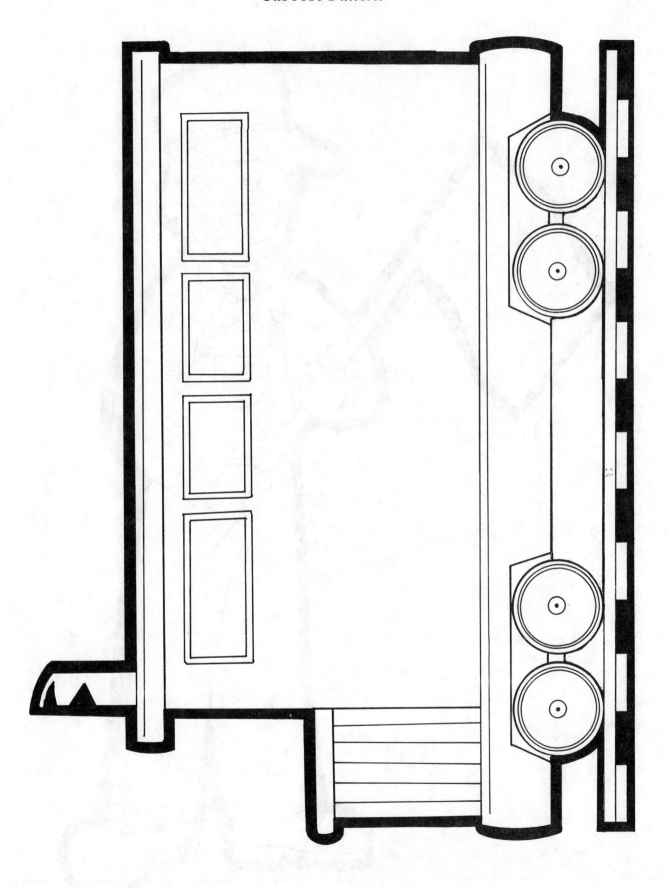

ROUNDING UP GOOD BEHAVIOR

Students can work towards a "Badge of Good Behavior" with this bulletin board. Display the patterns on pages 156 and 157 in the center of the board. Enlarge and personalize a badge pattern from page 159 for each student. Place all of the badges around the board. Each time a student is "caught being good," place a gold star on his badge.

Additional Uses

- List jobs on horses. Write student names on horseshoes. Display the horseshoes under the horses to match jobs and students.
- Graph students' favorite western animal – cow or horse. Display answers under copies of the cow and horse patterns.
- Study famous characters of the historical west. Display students' writings under the Cowboy and Cowgirl patterns.

Finishing Touches

- Use real rope for a lasso.
- Make stars out of aluminum foil.
- Use a bandana around the cowboy and cowgirl's necks.
- Bring in a cow bell and attach it to the bulletin board.
- Use a copper-colored pen to decorate the horseshoes.
- Cut out black cow spots and add them to the cow.

Creative Captions

- Trot On In
- Rootin' Tootin' Good Work
- Hitching Up to Math
- Rounding Up Good Behavior
- Racing to Read
- Hold Your Horses
- Get in the Writing "Moood"
- "Udderly" Fantastic
- Mr./Mrs. ___'s Shiny Deputies

Horse Pattern

159